P9-DUX-207

Pocket Reference Collection from IVP Academic

Pocket Dictionary for the Study of Biblical Hebrew by Todd J. Murphy
Pocket Dictionary for the Study of New Testament Greek by Matthew S. DeMoss
Pocket Dictionary of Apologetics & Philosophy of Religion by C. Stephen Evans
Pocket Dictionary of Biblical Studies by Arthur G. Patzia and Anthony J. Petrotta
Pocket Dictionary of Church History by Nathan P. Feldmeth
Pocket Dictionary of Ethics by Stanley J. Grenz and Jay T. Smith
Pocket Dictionary of New Religious Movements by Irving Hexham
Pocket Dictionary of North American Denominations by Drew Blankman and Todd Augustine
Pocket Dictionary of Theological Terms by Stanley J. Grenz, David Guretzki and Cherith Fee Nordling
Pocket Guide to World Religions by Winfried Corduan
Pocket Handbook of Christian Apologetics by Peter Kreeft and Ronald K. Tacelli
Pocket History of Evangelical Theology by Roger E. Olson
Pocket History of the Church by D. Jeffrey Bingham
Pocket History of Theology by Roger E. Olson and Adam C. English

POCKET DICTIONARY *of* ETHICS

Stanley J. Grenz
Jay T. Smith

InterVarsity Press
Downers Grove, Illinois

InterVarsity Press
P.O. Box 1400, Downers Grove, IL 60515-1426
www.ivpress.com
email@ivpress.com

InterVarsity Press® is the book-publishing division of InterVarsity Christian Fellowship/USA®, a movement of students and faculty active on campus at hundreds of universities, colleges, and schools of nursing in the United States of America, and a member movement of the International Fellowship of Evangelical Students. For information about local and regional activities, visit intervarsity.org.

Cover design: Kathleen Lay Burrows

Cover image: Roberta Polfus

ISBN 978-0-8308-1468-8

Printed in the United States of America ♾

InterVarsity Press is committed to ecological stewardship and to the conservation of natural resources in all our operations. This book was printed using sustainably sourced paper.

Library of Congress Cataloging-in-Publication Data

Grenz, Stanley, 1950-
Pocket dictionary of ethics / Stanley J. Grenz & Jay T. Smith.
p. cm.
Includes bibliographical references.
ISBN 0-8308-1468-X (pbk.: alk. paper)
1. Ethics—Dictionaries. I. Smith, Jay T. II. Title.
BJ63.G74 2003
170′.3—dc21

2003008233

P *24 23 22 21 20 19 18 17 16 15 14 13 12 11 10 9 8 7*

Y *35 34 33 32 31 30 29 28 27 26 25 24 23 22 21 20 19*

Preface

People today seem to be quite willing to speak the language of ethics. This may be due in part to the growing sense that we are being swamped with questions that at their core are ethical. But people appear also to be increasingly aware that questions of ethics are not merely "out there." On the contrary, we find ourselves bombarded with decisions about how we should live and what kind of persons we ought to be. And we realize that somehow what we do and who we are matters. Viewed from this perspective, we are all ethicists. This means that we are not given the luxury of asking, "Do I *want* to be an ethicist?" Rather, the crucial question is, "What *kind* of ethicist am I?"

Our ultimate goal in producing the *Pocket Dictionary of Ethics* is to assist you in becoming a good ethicist. We desire to contribute to this lofty goal by providing you with a tool for becoming a better-informed ethicist. To this end, what follows in these pages are short definitions or descriptions of some of the most important terms and names encountered in books and discussions in the broad field of ethics. These definitions are not exhaustive, of course, but are intended to provide a basic working knowledge of the central concepts bandied about in conversations about ethics. Rather than including concepts from a variety of religious and philosophical streams of thought, we have focused on the Greek, Western and Christian ethical traditions. We have also generally avoided terms that are limited to specialized subdisciplines, choosing instead concepts that frame the wider ethical discussion (including, we should forewarn you, one tongue-in-cheek entry). In this process, we have kept the number of entries dealing with individual ethicists to a minimum and have largely avoided twentieth- and twenty-first-century figures.

This little pocket dictionary is not meant to be read from cover to cover. Rather, it is intended to serve as a reference tool that you have on your desk as you read other books and essays on the topic. Nevertheless, you might consider reading through the book from *a* to *z* in order to gain a basic handle on the field of ethics in general. To facilitate its use as a reference tool, we have provided cross-references. An asterisk before a term or phrase indicates that it appears elsewhere in the book as a separate entry. *See* directs you to the entry where a term you have chosen is defined. *See also* indicates related entries in the pocket dictionary that provide additional information regarding the term you are exploring.

Finally, keep in mind that learning *about* ethics will not automatically result in your becoming a good ethicist. Knowledge must be applied—and, in the case of the quest to live ethically, applied under the direction of and with the empowerment of the Holy Spirit. Our prayer is that the *Pocket Dictionary of Ethics* might become a tool of the Spirit in effecting this greater goal in your life.

Stanley J. Grenz and Jay T. Smith

A

abortion. Any medical procedure that terminates the life of the human fetus prior to birth. Abortion loomed as one of the central ethical issues in the church and *society in the final four decades of the twentieth century. Connected to the question of abortion are such considerations as the *rights and welfare of the birth mother; the nature of *procreation and sexual activity; the value of unborn human life; and the interests of other parties, such as the father and other *family members. Some ethicists hold to one or the other of the two absolutist positions: "abortion on demand" or no abortion under any circumstances. Yet most of the ethical debate has centered on the question of the circumstances under which abortion might be deemed either morally permissible or the lesser of two evils (e.g., when the mother's life is endangered or in the case of rape). *See also* fetal research; life, right to.

absolute, absolutism. An ethical *principle or rule deemed universally obligatory, that is, binding on all persons and under all circumstances without exception. Ethical absolutism, in turn, is the theory that one or more ethical absolutes exist and can be discovered. Proponents of ethical absolutism differ among themselves regarding the source of such absolutes. Some suggest that they are rooted in the character of God and are given to humans by divine revelation. Others declare that moral absolutes are rooted in universal *human nature and are accessible through reason. *See also* nonconflicting absolutism; norm; universal moral judgments.

abstinence. As a general concept, abstinence denotes the act of refraining from a particular activity because of moral, religious or health convictions. As an ethical concept, it is most often used to denote the choice of an unmarried person to refrain from sexual activity, especially sexual intercourse. The validity of abstinence as the best stance for adolescent minors is widely debated today, as is abstinence-focused sex education in the public schools. *See also* sexuality, sexual ethics.

addiction. The condition of being given to habitual dependency. This dependency can manifest itself in various forms, such as substance addiction (*drugs, alcohol and stimulants), sexual addiction or activity addiction (shopping, spending, *gambling, Internet, television, etc.). Although many addictions are considered debilitating and even potentially harmful to the addict and to *society, discussions abound as to whether addiction is a medical/psychological or a moral category. That is, are addictions to be viewed as diseases or sins?

adultery. The act of sexual intercourse between a person who is married and someone who is not one's *marriage partner. The Old Testament expressly forbids adultery. The injunction against this practice is one of the Ten Commandments (Ex 20:14). Jesus not only repeated the commandment in his conversation with the rich young ruler (e.g., Mt 19:18), but in the *Sermon on the Mount applied it to the *lust of the heart (Mt 5:27-28). Contemporary discussions have raised the question as to whether the commandment against adultery extends to any physical contact of an explicitly sexual nature between two people who are not married. *See also* chastity.

advertising ethics. The study of the *standards of conduct that govern the process of informing the public about products and services. The ethical dimension of advertising arises from the fact that the practice is generally designed today to increase the demand for the products and services about which the public is being informed, thereby enhancing their perceived economic value and, in effect, creating or enhancing the desire for them. Advertising also raises the somewhat related ethical questions regarding the role of consumption in *society.

agape. A transliteration of a Greek word commonly translated into English as "*love." Agape, as an ethical concern, reflects its Hebrew cognate, *hesed,* in that it represents the self-denying value of lovingkindness, as reflected in God's love for creation. *Agape* is sometimes distinguished from the related Greek terms **eros* and *phileō,* which are also often translated into English as "love," but do not carry the idea of self-giving entailed in *agapē*. Many Christians have articulated what is often termed an agapeic ethic, that is, an approach to the ethical life that elevates love as the chief consideration. *See also* charity.

altruism. The selfless concern for the well-being of others. Some philosophical ethicists argue that altruistic concerns are present in every moral code and therefore that altruism belongs to the realm of naturalistic ethics (*see also* naturalism, ethical). Contemporary sociobiology offers a different kind of naturalistic understanding, claiming that altruism is connected to interest in the propagation of one's genes. Altruism as a motivation for conduct appears at the heart of Jesus' command to "*love your neighbor as yourself" (Lk 10:27). *See also* compassion.

analytical ethics. Derived from the term *analyze,* which means "to take things apart," analytical ethics is the branch of philosophical or *general ethics that explores the nature of *morality itself. Analytical ethicists attempt to develop a theory as to what *value judgments mean and how they can be justified. Sometimes the term is used synonymously with **metaethics.*

animal rights. The set of moral *obligations that nonhuman animals can demand from humans or that humans owe to animals, especially the *principle that animals have legitimate claims to humane, equitable treatment. Animal rights proponents generally presuppose one of two foundational views: that animals, as part of the created order, are entitled to merciful and compassionate treatment from humans, or that humans are simply another species in the animal kingdom and as such have no moral primacy over the rest of the animal kingdom. The concept of animal *rights is a relatively new development. Stephen Clark, Mary Midgely, Tom Regan and Peter Singer are among the contemporary voices calling for a concern for the rights of animals.

anti-Semitism. The condition of being characterized by prejudicial attitudes and actions against the Jewish people in general or individual Jews merely on the basis of their ethnicity. Anti-Semitism emerges as a special problem for Christian theology and *Christian ethics due to the unique historical and theological relationship between Christianity and the Jewish faith. *See also* discrimination; prejudice; racism.

antinomianism. Literally, "against or in opposition to, the *law." Antinomianism as a Christian theological term asserts that grace through *faith has abolished the law (Gal 3:11; Eph 2:8-9), and that therefore the Christian is no longer subject to the law in any sense. Taken to an extreme, antinomianism leads to licentious if not ethically questionable conduct. That it was a problem in the early church is evident by the repeated warnings against it found in several New Testament writings.

anxiety, ethical. A feeling of despair brought on by the necessity to make ethical or moral decisions. Ethical anxiety is a necessary attribute in the formation of moral *character in the ethical *society. Søren *Kierkegaard asserted that anxiety was one of the markers of true *freedom of choice.

apartheid. A term initially arising from South Africa that literally means "apartness." It is usually understood in the context of racial segregation, and more particularly to the racial policies of the South African government from 1950 through 1991. As an ethical term, apartheid may be used to refer to any perceived immoral separation of elements to the point that one element is excluded for the sake of the benefit of the other. Hence, in human social relations, it denotes the separation of one group from another for the sake of enhancing the status of members of the one group, possibly at the expense of the others in *society. *See also* discrimination; racism.

Aquinas, Thomas. *See* Thomas Aquinas.

Aristotle. An ancient Greek philosopher credited with being the first thinker in Western civilization to offer a systematic treatise on *ethics, his *Nicomachean Ethics.* Aristotle (384-323 B.C.) was a student of *Plato, became the tutor of Alexander the Great and later founded his own school, the Lyceum. Aristotle's view of metaphysics is foundational to moral reflection. Ethics begins with the search for the highest human *good, which is *happiness, understood as well-being rather than as a psychological state. This happiness is tied to human functioning and as such consists of a life of virtuous activity lived in accordance to reason. Moral *virtues are acquired through the rational control of desires and involve a deliberate concern to fulfill our "end" or highest good. Aristotelian ethics, in turn, are framed by the human pursuit of the final cause appropriate to human life, which is the highest human good. *See also* golden mean.

armaments. The military equipment and personnel of a nation, group or individual. Although armaments include the personnel that carry out the tactical and strategic military aims of a nation, the term is generally used in a narrower sense to refer to the equipment available for use in warfare or a combat situation. This equipment may range from simple hand-held weapons, such as knives, to complex nuclear explosives and their delivery mechanisms. The ethical questions regarding armaments are connected to the *morality of the use of physical *force in general and warfare in particular to resolve problems. *See also* disarmament; nuclear warfare.

artificial insemination. The designation of a variety of commonly used means to assist the reproductive process in which a concentrated amount of semen is introduced into the female ovum in a clinical environment. Among married couples, artificial insemination is usually pursued when an abnormality greatly reduces the possibility of conception by sexual intercourse. Artificial insemination by the husband (AIH) is the least controversial variety of this method of artificial conception. Artificial insemination by a donor (AID), often pursued when the husband does not have viable sperm or is a carrier of a possible genetic disorder, is more controversial, in that the child produced by this method will have no genetic link to the husband of the mother. Artificial insemination by donor is frequently criticized in religious circles as an attack on God's sovereignty over creation or on God's intention for *marriage. AID is also deemed suspect in that it facilitates a single woman's producing a child. *See also* genetics, genetic engineering; procreation; reproductive technologies.

asylum. As a political term, the protection granted by one country to *refugees from another country, usually in response to political, ethnic or religious *persecution. Ethical issues connected with asylum include such matters as asylum as a right, the conditions under which the granting of asylum is a moral *duty, the link between *justice (including *distributive justice) and the practice of asylum, and humane treatment of asylum seekers. In medical parlance, an asylum is an institution dedicated to the treatment of the mentally ill. Today ethical questions are being raised regarding the proper treatment of mental patients, including whether placing persons in asylums can be justified morally.

Augustine (A.D. 354-430). A North African convert to Christianity hailed as one of the greatest theologians in the history of the church. At the heart of Augustine's thought was his appropriation of a Neo-Platonic ontology (*see* Neo-Platonism) that viewed being as forming a kind of hierarchy, at the apex of which was the "One," the fullness of being. The One was also an ethical concept in that it was held to be the perfect *good. Augustine linked the Neo-Platonic One to the Christian God, who is also the highest good. Therefore, Augustine asserted that the human **summum bonum* is God, or better, the enjoyment of God. On this foundation, Augustine constructed his understanding of the Christian ethic, which he viewed as an ethic based on God's *love for us, which moves our *will and thereby evokes in us love for God.

autonomy. Literally, "self *law" or "self rule," and hence the independent exercise of an individual or community's *will leading to moral claims that are seen to be determined by the individual. In general, autonomy—which is often viewed as the opposite of *heteronomy and is sometimes contrasted to *theonomy—entails the rejection of all moral claims deemed to arise from a source that is external to the individual or *community or to which the individual or community does not have direct access. *See also* freedom; individualism; moral autonomy.

avarice. A synonym for *greed. Avarice is a preoccupation with the accumulation of material *wealth, especially wealth in abundance that is hoarded for the sake of one's own benefit. Avarice is often associated with immoral behaviors (e.g., embezzlement, fraud and simple theft) connected to this preoccupation. But the ethical questions it raises move beyond particular immoral conduct to include issues of *justice—at what point is the accumulation of *wealth, even by ethical means, immoral?—and the nature of the *good life.

B

beatitude. An ancient literary form used to describe the blessed nature of the life that is lived within the parameters of God's expectations. In extolling certain ways of living as blessed, a beatitude prescribes such behaviors for, or commends such ways of living to, others. The most famous collection of beatitudes were spoken by Jesus in his *Sermon on the Mount (Mt 5:3-10), a text that has repeatedly formed part of the core of proposals of *Christian ethics.

beneficence. The act of well-doing, or the *obligation of doing *good to others. Most ethical theorists teach beneficence. In the

New Testament, beneficence is often enjoined on Christians by appeal to the example of Jesus or to God's ways of dealing with creatures. Jesus cited God's goodness in causing the sun to shine on *righteous as well as unrighteous persons as indicating the kind of beneficence that ought to characterize his followers. *See also* benevolence.

benevolence. The attitude of intending or the action of doing *good toward others. Benevolence, as a disposition of the *will, is subjective. As a subjective disposition, benevolence is considered to correspond to the activity of *beneficence. *See also* charity.

bestiality. The act of sexual intercourse between a human and an animal. This relationship is considered scientifically dysfunctional and morally reprehensible in most, if not all civilizations. Injunctions against bestiality are found in the holiness codes of the Pentateuch (Ex 22:19; Lev 18:23; 20:5-16; Deut 27:21). Some contemporary ethicists condemn such conduct not only as a violation of human *sexuality but also as an affront to the rights of animals (*see* animal rights), who ought not to be misused in this manner for human pleasure.

bigamy. The condition of being married to two spouses simultaneously. Hence it includes the situation in which a person marries while a previous *marriage is still legally binding. Although this practice is illegal in Western countries influenced by Christianity, people groups in other parts of the world (as well as some sects associated with Christianity) commonly practice bigamy or *polygamy. *See also* monogamy.

bioethics. The application of ethics to the fields of biological science, including medicine, *genetics and related areas. The use of the term is relatively recent, with one of its earliest appearances being in V. R. Potter's book *Bioethics: Bridge to the Future* (1971). Many researchers see the contents of this field as more appropriately identified under the rubric biomedical ethics; yet the term *bioethics* is still the more common identifier. *See also* medical ethics; reproductive technologies.

biological warfare. The intentional use of toxic microorganisms in military actions. Agents such as smallpox or anthrax have been utilized in producing weapons of this type. The use of biological weapons was banned by the Geneva Conventions. Even just war theorists, that is, ethicists who defend the practice of *war under certain circumstances (*see* just war theory), generally find the use of biological weapons reprehensible when judged by the *standards of what constitutes a just war.

birth control. The restriction or limitation of *procreation by choice. Christians have long debated the moral status of birth control. Some argue that it interferes with God's sovereign intention in the conjugal act, whereas others affirm it as a means to practice good *stewardship of one's reproductive capabilities. The debate has been exacerbated by the invention of newer birth control techniques that now often replace the older, so-called natural methods. Some of these methods entail the use of a physical barrier or substance that prevents conception. Even more questionable in the eyes of many ethicists are those methods that prevent pregnancy after fertilization has occurred. *See also* contraception, contraceptives.

bisexuality. The condition of being sexually aroused by persons of both sexes. Some ethicists argue against bisexuality on the basis of its link to *homosexuality. Although defenders of homosexuality have increasingly included bisexuality within their advocacy activities, many homosexual persons condemn bisexuality as being an affront to what is believed to be a person's fixed sexual orientation.

blasphemy. A transliteration of the Greek term *blasphēmia,* meaning "*slander, revile." In the Bible, the term *blasphemy* is used describe the act of intentionally or carelessly profaning God. The Old Testament understood blasphemy as a serious *sin, punishable in death by stoning (Lev 24:13-16). Although not mentioning the death penalty, the New Testament writers affirmed the seriousness of blasphemy as a sin. Jesus expanded the idea to include blasphemy against the Holy Spirit, for which there is no *forgiveness (Mt 12:31). In ethical discourse, blasphemy is related to the wider question of proper speech, a category that includes a variety of practices, including *oaths.

blue laws. A series of legal statutes that prohibits forms of entertainment and most commercial establishments from conducting business on Sunday. In the United States, blue laws originated in *Puritan New England and derived their name from the blue paper upon which they were printed. Their biblical basis lay in the Sabbath-keeping laws of the Old Testament. Most blue laws were repealed in the United States in the twentieth century. *See also* Sabbatarianism; Sunday laws.

bribery. The act of receiving or giving an inducement to perform a service that is presumed to be free of secretive solicitation. A bribe is usually an offer of money, goods or services in exchange for the illicit service. Bribes are seen as unethical insofar as they improperly influence the performances of services that are usually exercised for the benefit of the public at large. The Christian tradition consistently condemns the offering of bribes. Yet bribery is a common practice in many parts of the world. This has led some ethicists to conclude that the moral status of such acts are dependent on the cultural context and social mores in which they occur. Other ethicists conclude that in certain cultures giving a bribe may at times actually be the lesser of two evils.

business ethics. The application of ethical categories to the unique positions and responsibilities within the contemporary business enterprise. The rise of specific business entities within capitalist *society, such as corporations, professional management, stockholders, unions and entrepreneurs has created a need to develop a moral agency with which to deal with the issues endemic to Western market economies. The application of Christian ethical teaching to these areas has been slow, due in part to the perception that its dominant focus is on individual ethical *responsibility. Nevertheless, the advent of the corporate entity in Western culture has occasioned an interest among many Christian ethicists (*see* Christian ethics) to expand their moral reflection to both the ethical dimensions of the conduct of business, as well as the implications of the social inequalities brought about by capitalism. *See also* corporate responsibility; economic system; employment; industrial ethics; labor ethics; professional ethics; whistle-blowing.

C

calumny. A false or malicious statement issued with the intent to do *harm to a person's character or reputation. Calumny is *slander. Insofar as it entails the defamation of character, it becomes the grounds for potential legal action.

canon law. The body of rules established by ecclesial bodies for the government of their internal relationships and the conduct—including the ethical conduct—of their members. In Christian circles, canon law is codified and utilized primarily by the Roman Catholic Church (*see also* encyclicals), the Eastern Orthodox Church and the Church of England. Some proponents suggest that canon law initially arose in the New Testament era as the Jerusalem church formed the apostolic college in order to establish some general theological and ethical guidelines for believers everywhere (Acts 15). These rules grew throughout the first century until they were eventually codified by the Western church in the *Corpus iuris canonici.* The term "canon law," as an expression of ecclesial rules, is generally not used by Protestants.

capital punishment. The legal execution of an individual as the penalty for a *crime, usually *murder or sedition. Capital punishment has pre-Christian origins. In the modern era, it has come under sharp criticism by many ethicists who condemn it as an inhumane *punishment. Christians are divided on capital punishment, some supporting it on the basis of a variety of considerations including Old Testament practice, and others rejecting it as a violation of the biblical injunction against murder. *See also* penology.

cardinal virtues. A term used especially in *virtue ethics to refer to the central or principle character traits that lie at the heart of, or promote, the *good life. *Plato spoke about four principle virtues that he saw as being related to the three functions (or perhaps "parts") of the soul. Thus, *wisdom corresponded to reason, *courage to spirit or *will, and *temperance to desire or appetite, with *justice forming the integrative virtue. Sometimes the Greek cardinal virtues are listed as *prudence, justice, temperance and *fortitude. As a Christian ethicist, *Thomas Aquinas accepted these four but believed that they were to be subordinate to the three *theological virtues of *faith, hope and *love.

casuistry. Linked to the idea of "case law," casuistry refers to any form of argument about moral or legal issues that argues from the abstract to the particular. Casuistry seeks, then, to apply abstract or universal moral *principles to particular, unique cases (*see also* universal moral judgments). Ethicists often claim that casuistry is found in the New Testament, such as in Paul's attempt to apply Christian principles to the question of eating meat that had been sacrificed to idols (1 Cor 8). Casuistry as a form of moral argument developed in the late Middle Ages as a means of assisting priests as they served as confessors. Some adherents of *situation ethics reject casuistry on the basis of the uniqueness of every ethical *decision-making context. *See also* probabilism.

categorical imperative. The designation of the supreme *principle of *duty, according to certain ethicists in the tradition of *deontological ethics but especially Immanuel *Kant. Kant offered several formulations of the categorical imperative, the most important of which states, "Act in conformity with that maxim, and that maxim only, that you can will at the same time to be a universal law" (*see also* universal moral judgments). Hence, for Kant, right actions flow out of right principles, and right principles in turn govern, at least in theory, situations. In any situation, Kant advised, do the act that is motivated by the sincere belief that what you are doing is the *right thing to do not merely for you, but for anybody seeking to act properly in any similar situation. A second form of the categorical imperative focuses more on the treatment of others: "Act in such a way that you always treat humans not merely as a means to an end but also as an end." *See also* imperative; rule-deontologism.

celibacy. The state of willfully choosing to be unmarried and, more specifically, not to engage in physical sexual activity. Although the term is often used in the general sense to refer to anyone who willingly chooses *abstinence, celibacy carries the more technical sense of this choice being motivated by a sense of religious vocation, *obligation or *duty. In Christian history, a central ethical question involves mandated celibacy for clergy. In the patristic era, church leaders extolled the superiority of celibacy over *marriage, especially for priests and bishops, and this eventually led to the inclusion of a vow of celibacy in church ordination practices, which the Reformers later opposed (*see also* patristic ethics; Reformation ethics). The biblical basis for celibacy includes Paul's assertion that being single has certain advantages for service in that a single person is undivided in his or her devotion to the Lord (1 Cor 7:32-35).

censorship. The examination and abridgment of media content before it is broadcast or published in order to prevent what are considered undesirable elements from public consumption. In contemporary culture, censorship has been invoked primarily over the issue of *pornography, although historically it has also been used to edit religious or political materials. Current discussions regarding the ethics of censorship tend to pit individual *rights, such as free speech and self-expression, against considerations of the potential *harm to other individuals as well as the general social good (i.e., the *common good).

character. The various dimensions of personality, either natural or acquired, that distinguish one individual from another. As an ethical term, character refers to the traits of an individual that may be deemed morally blameworthy or praiseworthy. The term is often used in a positive sense to refer to the possession of virtues that result in a person being lauded as morally upright or that are believed to foster *right actions. In classical ethics, character was believed to be the product of the practice of specific *virtues or *vices, or the formation of moral *habits. Contemporary ethicists generally maintain that character also includes the capacity for intentional action or simply the ability to reason and choose, which, in turn, endows a person with moral and social *responsibility for one's own actions. *Christian ethics tends to look to Jesus Christ as the standard for character and suggests that character stems from a life of *faith in Jesus Christ. Additionally, Christians posit that character is developed within the faith *community or church. *See also* integrity.

charity. The social embodiment of the *love of God for the love of neighbor. Although the term arises from the Latin word *caritas,* which is a translation of the Greek *agapē,* charity has come to be associated with acts of *benevolence in response to human social needs. *See also* agape.

chastity. The preservation of sexual purity. Although the term refers to sexual *integrity in general, whether as a married or a single person, chastity is often understood in the narrower sense of preserving one's virginity. The violation of chastity, that is, engaging in sexual relations outside of *marriage, is called *fornication in the case of unmarried persons and *adultery when it involves a married individual. As a *virtue, chastity is sometimes seen as including not only sexual purity, but also the desire to embody the *love of God in relationships with others.

cheating. The practice of fraud or deception with the *intention of personal gain. Cheating can also be understood as unfaithfulness to one's marital partner. A person who practices deception for personal gain is called a cheat.

child abuse. The intentional or unintentional neglect of a child's most basic needs for protection, *love and physical necessities such as food, shelter and clothing, by a person who stands in a relationship of trust to, or carries *responsibility toward the child. In its most severe forms, child abuse includes such overt acts as sexual impropriety (e.g., rape, *incest), harsh physical treatment resulting in disfigurement or disability, and harsh verbal or mental treatment resulting in long-term personality dysfunction.

Christian ethics. The study of how humans ought to live as informed by the Bible, Christian tradition and Christian convictions. Christian ethics attempts to describe how Christian convictions and teachings regarding God's relationship with the world and particularly with human beings ought to inform the conception of the moral life and influence moral choices (*see also* morality, morals). *See also* evangelical ethics; New Testament ethics.

church and state. A phrase used to denote the relationship between the ecclesial organizations and the civil government of *society, or between the religious and the political dimensions of life especially as they are embodied in organized visible forms. Insofar as both of these institutions or dimensions of life claim allegiance from humans, the relationship between the two has become increasingly important to define, especially in nontheocratic societies. In countries where religious *freedom is protected, under certain circumstances allegiance to one abrogates allegiance to the other or is seen as coinciding with allegiance to the other. The coincidence of church and state is best illustrated in the contemporary world by the Islamic state and in Western history by the Holy Roman Empire.

civil disobedience. An act of protest in which citizens dissent from established governmental policy. This form of protest has spawned debate as to what acts of disobedience are justifiable and under what conditions dissent can be carried out. The term "civil disobedience" is often attributed to Henry David Thoreau and his 1849 essay "Civil Disobedience." In contemporary history, both Mahatma Gandhi in India and Martin Luther King Jr. in the United

States pursued acts of civil disobedience in order to secure humanitarian goals. *See also* nonviolence.

civil rights. The legal *rights of the citizens of a state. Civil rights are differentiated from both *human rights and *natural rights in that they are protected and enforced by law. Civil rights are coterminous with both human rights and natural rights to the extent that they are generally viewed as arising out of convictions about human rights, natural rights or both.

cloning. The *reproductive technology that produces a genetically identical duplicate of an organism by nuclear cellular manipulation. In this process, the nucleus of an unfertilized ovum is replaced with the nucleus of a body cell from the same species. Those who question the ethical legitimacy of human cloning include both Christian and secular ethicists, some of whom argue against the practice on the basis of its perceived assault on the dignity and uniqueness of the individual human person. *See also* fetal research; life, sanctity of; technological ethics.

cohabitation. The circumstance in which an unmarried couple share a residence and engage in regular sexual intimacy, including intercourse. Many in *Christian ethics argue that cohabitation is consistently condemned in the Bible, insofar as it fails to reflect the normative process by which the marital relationship is inaugurated, including the public act of covenanting with one another to be husband and wife to each other. Some ethicists add that cohabitation involves a weaker bond than that of publicly declared *marriage, and they point out that cohabitation carries a greater potential for such ills as spouse abuse, *adultery and *divorce.

collectivism. The theory that *property—especially land or other means of production—ought to be owned by groups of people rather than individuals. Collectivism is an underlying tenet of *socialism. It is often viewed as the opposite of *individualism and, by extension, is used to denote the practice of any *society in which group structures exercise overt control over individuals. *See also* Marxism.

comfortism. A contemporary school of ethical thought that determines *right actions by asking, "Are you/am I comfortable with this?" Proponents see their view as the ethical outworking of Jesus' promise that his yoke would be easy and his burden light. If a proposed action is not favorable to comfort, advocates add, it should be adjusted until it is. Comfortists point out that they stand in a long and distinguished tradition that can boast many notable exemplars. Critics contend that comfort is not a proper ethical category, a perspective they derive from sayings of Jesus, such as the necessity of taking up one's cross and following him, which comfortists tend to view as either hyperbolic or inauthentic.

commandments. Orders, injunctions or precepts that are considered authoritative. For many Jews and Christians the chief of these are the Ten Commandments or the Decalogue, as recorded in Exodus 20:1-17 and Deuteronomy 5:6-21. These commandments have been observed throughout the history of the church as an exposition of God's requirements for ethical behavior.

common good. The idea that the normative standard for evaluating the *justice inherent within legal, social and political actions is the *good of the people as a whole or, perhaps, of each person within *society. To the extent that an act benefits the *community in its entirety or everyone in the community, it is regarded to be "for the common good." The common good is both a goal to be achieved and a source of fulfillment once attained. Though the concept of common good has its roots in antiquity, its full formulation is credited to *Thomistic ethics and Neo-Thomistic ethics. The term has also been linked to *utilitarianism and has been understood antithetically to Jeremy Bentham's concept of the "greatest good."

common-law marriage. The formation of a marital relationship by means of explicit or implicit mutual *consent, exclusive of either civil or religious contractual commitment. In most Western societies today a common-law *marriage has come to be considered a legal union, thereby legitimizing the children born from it and protecting the *rights of the individuals involved.

community. A group of persons that consciously or unconsciously share one or more normative designations that are spatial, political, ethnic, moral or spiritual. A community may be geographically based, such as a city or neighborhood. However, a community may be formed by other commonalities, such as shared ethnicity. In contemporary religious thought, the term also designates a group bound together by a strong commitment to shared spiritual values and a common sense of being a people who embody a *telos,* or purpose, connected to God's intentions for humankind and creation. *See also koinonia.*

compassion. An attitude or emotion that is altruistic in nature and therefore leads to selfless acts of *beneficence on behalf of another. Compassion presupposes such dispositions as *sympathy and mercy. Christianity has long championed the cultivation of compassion as one of its core moral *imperatives. *See also* altruism.

computer ethics. The branch of the ethical discipline that seeks to apply ethical *standards of conduct to the use of computer technology. Computers, as inanimate machines, have no inherent ethical predisposition. However, the use of computer technology to engage in questionable moral pursuits and to participate in illegal activity is becoming more prevalent. Additionally, some ethicists assert that the possession of a computer and the use of its technology implies a certain hegemony of control over information that marginalizes those who do not have such access. *See also* cybernetics; technological ethics; virtual sex.

concupiscence. The inordinate and inappropriate desire for something. Often the term is connected to illicit sexual desires or an overvaluing of sexual pleasure. Yet concupiscence can also be used to refer to such ills as overeating or substance abuse. Inordinate desires are generally seen as stemming from and an indication of underlying psychological or spiritual maladies.

confidentiality. The situation in which a relationship of trust is created so that one person is enabled to disclose information to another with the understanding that the recipient not disseminate it further. The term is used particularly to designate relationships between clients and those in the legal, medical, counseling, social work and ministerial professions. In these relationships, clients disclose information that could have negative effects on themselves or others if it were divulged to those not yet privy to it. *See also* privacy; professional ethics.

conflict of interest. A situation in which a person has an ethical *obligation to perform two or more duties that appear to be mutually exclusive. Often in such a situation, the individual is faced with the decision as to which obligation must take ethical priority.

conscience. The inner witness to moral *responsibility or the inherent human ability or capacity to discern *good and *evil, *right and wrong, as well as to sense *guilt when moral codes are transgressed. Although generally used with reference to individuals, the term also carries a metaphorical meaning when it refers to a person who is viewed as acting as the conscience of a nation or *society. On the basis of several biblical texts (e.g., Rom 2:14-15), many Christian ethicists view the possession of a conscience as part of God's general revelation or *beneficence to humankind, albeit one that leads to human guilt before God. Consequently, conscience is not sufficient for attaining a moral life; to it must be added special revelation and divine assistance. *See also* synderesis.

conscientious objection. The refusal to participate in activities that are contrary to one's ethical beliefs. In its general sense, conscientious objection denotes any form of protest against institutional rules or government laws. Most often the term is used more narrowly, however, to refer to the refusal to participate in military service on humanitarian or religious grounds. *See also* pacifism.

consent. An act of voluntary agreement or assent to a proposed act. Consent transfers the *rights and responsibilities of the one who consents to another agent. Because consent may not actually imply complete agreement, it may be given reluctantly. At the same time, its voluntary nature means that agreement given under duress or coercion is not true consent. In *ethics, the principle of *informed consent means that a person can be deemed to have granted consent only if he or she has been adequately informed as to the nature, risks, benefits and alternatives, thereby facilitating the making of an uncoerced decision.

consequentialism. *See* teleological ethics.

contraception, contraceptives. The physical or chemical means that prevents embryonic conception from resulting from sexual intercourse. Although technically the term refers only to those procedures that prevent conception, it is often used to denote any means of *birth control that employs manufactured aids, including those that prevent pregnancy after conception has occurred. *Christian ethics has debated contraception as a particular type of birth control, in part because of the manipulation it asserts over the procreative process (*see* procreation) and because of the belief that its use carries a propensity to encourage sexual *sin (*see* sexuality, sexual ethics). Until recently, the Roman Catholic Church has banned contraceptive devices, while favoring so-called natural forms of birth control. *See also* sterilization.

contracts. Voluntary agreements between two or more parties that create legal *obligations for the parties involved. Contracts are important in free market economies insofar as individual *rights and freedoms necessitate such binding agreements.

conventionalism. The belief that moral *standards are the product of communal conventions. According to this theory, a *community determines its own rules of conduct in accordance with its own *customs (or conventions), which in turn are based on its unique vision of reality. *See also* pluralism; relativism.

copyright. The possession of the legal right to control a piece of intellectual, artistic or literary material. Generally a copyright entails a legal protection of published materials (transmitted through a variety of media) that guarantees to either the creators of the materials or others acting on their behalf control over their product. This control extends to the distribution, reduplication, performance and collection of profits generated by the materials. Under certain circumstances, notably limited scholarly use, copyrighted works may be quoted without permission or penalty. In an increasingly complex world, what constitutes the infringement of the copyright is constantly debated.

corporal punishment. The act of disciplining an individual in a way that seeks to create a degree of physical pain in order to extract *obedience or correct deviant behavior. The level of pain inflicted varies from mild to extreme, usually administered proportionately to the offense being corrected. Advocates of the use of corporal punishment in the discipline of a child by a parent or other authority generally agree that in most cases such acts ought to be limited to ones that inflict a mild amount of pain, such as spanking. Corporal punishment in the extreme may be considered torture and can even cause death. Opponents of corporal punishment argue that such *punishment is inhumane and abusive, or they question its viability as acceptable means for correcting individual behavior.

corporate responsibility. The accountability of people groups as a whole, such as political organizations, business organizations or nonprofit organizations including religious institutions, for their legal, financial and ethical acts. According to the concept of corporate *responsibility, these organized groups, or corporations, have responsibilities similar to those of individual human persons, and as a result, the mission or purpose of any organization carries ethical *obligations toward *society as a whole. The organization should conduct its business in a manner that evidences these ethical obligations. *See also* business ethics.

courage. A *virtue that entails the capability to endure, resist or alter adversity. Together with *wisdom, *justice and *temperance, *courage (or *fortitude)—defined as the ability to act according to reason in the face of fear—is numbered among the four *cardinal virtues of ancient Greek thought. The Bible enjoins a courage that goes beyond the mere managing of one's fears, for the exercise of this virtue arises out of confidence in God.

crime, criminality. As a civil or legal concept, an act that is committed in violation of a public *law or statute that prohibits precisely such an act. *Crime* may also be used as the collective designation of such violations. Criminality, in turn, is the quality of being oriented toward committing crime. Linked with the concept of crime is the idea of "victim," that is, the person or people directly affected by a crime, as well as the idea of "victimless crimes." As a religious concept, crime denotes an act that violates a moral law, command or injunction; it is a moral transgression or, stated simply, a *sin. Because Christians believe that the propensity to commit sins is a universal human characteristic, crime is an *evil that will be present in all societies.

cultural mandate. The teaching of some Christian traditions that human beings have received from God an innate impulse toward cultural development and, as a consequence, that such development comes under the purview of God's purposes for human *society and ultimately God's laws. Hence, the idea of the cultural mandate leads ethicists to seek to determine the implications of biblical teachings, divine commands in the Bible, and the biblical understanding of human social existence for the creation and function of human society. The concept of the divine mandate is often connected with the Calvinist tradition, and it is also found in the ethical works of Emil Brunner and Reinhold Niebuhr.

custom. A habitual pattern of behavior that is characteristic of a specific social group. Customs are developed in response to the context in which the social group maintains its existence, and they reflect the values that the social group holds to be normative. *See also* habit; norm.

cybernetics. The science of control and communication as it relates to mechanisms, individuals and societies. It is derived from the Greek term *kybernētēs*, which means "steersman." Cybernetics includes the various types of processes that depend on the exchange and flow of information. A cybernetic device is a mechanism or system that processes information, such as a computer or telecommunications system. The study of cybernetics raises a number of ethical questions, foremost of which is the development of artificial intelligence and its implications for what it means to be a living being. *See also* computer ethics; robotics; technological ethics.

Cynicism. An ancient school of ethical thought that held that all human behavior is motivated by selfish desire, but that *goodness is the highest attainment in life, so a person must aspire to *virtue in order to achieve *happiness. The Cynics taught that virtue can only be attained by the application of the mind to the task of achieving complete self-sufficiency and independence from the material. They also eschewed *wealth and asserted that *pleasure is the supreme enemy of life. The most notable Cynic, Diogenes of Sinope (fourth century B.C.), renounced civilization and called for a return to the simple life. In renouncing the world, Cynics were known to do private acts in public, believing that if something was *right, it could be done anywhere.

D

death. The cessation of the biological processes by which life is maintained. In modern medical parlance, death is defined by the loss of all brain functions, which leads to the decay of the organism itself. In the eyes of many people today, insofar as death marks the end of biologically animate living, it is to be postponed or avoided at all cost. In most world religions, death carries deeper meanings as well. Death is universal and inevitable, yet it is not necessarily the ultimate end of life. According to Christian teaching, death refers to ultimate alienation from God, since human beings are created for life in eternal community with God, creation and one another. The Christian gospel promises eternal life for all who believe in Jesus Christ. This promise helps to remove the fear of death by sustaining the hope of the ability to transcend death through the resurrection power of God. Death has emerged as a topic of ethical discussion, especially as it is connected with issues such as *euthanasia. *See also* life, quality of; life, sanctity of.

decision making. The process whereby an individual or *community chooses a particular course of action that results in specific outcomes. For most people or societies, decision making is guided by a fluctuating set of values, goals, moral *obligations and historical precedence. Many ethicists understand the ethical task to be the making of *right decisions; hence, they advocate what might be called an *ethic of doing. Moreover, ethicists since *Socrates have debated two basic approaches to ethical decision making: *deontological ethics and *teleological ethics. The deontological approach suggests that rightness or wrongness of an act is to be determined by something intrinsic to the act, whereas the teleological approach argues that the consequences of an act determine its moral status.

deontological ethics. The method of moral reasoning that asserts that the moral propriety of an act resides entirely in the act, being somehow connected to what is intrinsic to the act itself, and is not dependent upon the intent or the motive of the doer (*see also* intention). There are several forms of deontological ethics, including act-deontologism and *rule-deontologism. The rule-deontological approach suggests that moral behavior should be determined by one or more rules that govern all actions and all situations. Advocates differ over the number of such rules and how moral reasoning ought to proceed in a situation in which two or more rules are in conflict (such as the conflict between truth-telling and the protection of innocent persons evidenced in the biblical story of Rahab [Josh 2]). Immanuel *Kant popularized a monistic form of rule-deontologism with his articulation of the *categorical imperative.

depravity. *See* total depravity.

determinism. Generally defined in opposition to the concept of *free will, *determinism, as it relates to *ethics, asserts that all human behaviors are the necessary or inevitable result of prior causes. Natural determinism sees all events as a direct result of prior causes in a chain of cause and effect present throughout the universe. Theological determinism asserts that God directly or indirectly causes all events. Many ethicists reject both forms of determinism on the assumption that neither allows for the possibility of free human choice, which is foundational for moral *responsibility.

dialectical ethics. Any ethical philosophy whose principles for the interpretation of the moral life point to conflicting elements that are to be held in tension. The heart of dialectical ethics lies in the paradox between assertion and counterassertion. A dialectical ethic, therefore, emerges in the tension that exists between two or more ethical propositions. Perhaps one of the foremost examples of the operation of the dialectical approach is in the response to the presumed conflict between *determinism and *free will in which the truth is said to lie in the tension between these two aspects of the human reality. Though the concept of dialectic thought can be traced back to *Plato, the use of dialectic reaches a plateau with G. F. W. Hegel and Søren *Kierkegaard. Hegel believed that history flowed through an ongoing dialectical process in which opposing *principles were taken up in a higher synthesis. Kierkegaard asserted that the Christian dialectic does not find a resolution in synthesis but in paradox, a paradox that is grasped only in *faith. Some Christian ethicists take a cautious stance toward the dialectical approach on the basis of their commitment to Scripture as normative guide.

disarmament. The control, reduction and elimination of the weapons of *war and mass destruction. Disarmament can be forced, as by the victor of a war on the vanquished; it can be undertaken unilaterally for moral reasons; and it can be the result of a negotiated agreement. The ethical discussion has tended to focus on the question of the validity of unilateral disarmament. Many Christians believe that the Christian commitment to *peace affirms such a course of action as a moral necessity, whereas others advocate "peace through strength." *See also* armaments; pacifism.

discrimination. The drawing of distinctions between persons or groups that results in treating one or more of the persons or groups less favorably than others. Discrimination can be intentional or unintentional. Although the term can carry the positive connotation of practicing discernment or drawing fine distinctions, with regard to ethical matters it is generally used in the negative sense, namely, referring to actions and policies that treat persons or groups unjustly on the basis of some factor, such as sex, ethnicity or age. Discrimination in the sense of showing partiality is condemned in the New Testament, in part on the basis of God's impartial way of acting toward humans (e.g., Mt 5:45). *See also* feminist ethics; prejudice; racism.

distributive justice. The aspect of *justice that is concerned with the distribution of benefits, burdens and *rights in a *community. At the heart of the concern for distributive justice is the adequate, fair and equitable appropriation and distribution of goods and services within a particular *society. In addition, distributive justice considers the whole in relation to its constituent parts. As a consequence, it entails not only the distribution of the benefits but the equitable distribution of the burdens, such as taxation and military service. In *ethics, distributive justice is related to *social justice, as well as *human rights and *civil rights.

divine command theory. *See* theological voluntarism.

divorce. The legal termination of the marital relationship, which, at least in most societies today, includes the right to marry another. Although the Bible teaches that *marriage is to be a lifelong commitment, it acknowledges that divorce does occur. Exegetes and ethicists are not of one mind as to what constitutes valid biblical grounds for divorce. Some point to reasons such as "indecency" (Deut 24:1 RSV), *adultery (Mt 19:9) and desertion (1 Cor 7:15). Others claim that divorce is never justifiable (Mk 10:11-12), and if divorce occurs the divorced person ought not to marry a second time (1 Cor 7:11).

double effect. The theory that a moral agent is not to be held morally accountable for unintended and perhaps unavoidable ill side effects of an action or series of actions that is otherwise morally legitimate. Some ethicists add that the *principle of double effect can only be invoked in situations in which the *good intended in the action or series of acts is so significant that it outweighs the unintended evil side effect. Some antiabortionists have appealed to the principle of double effect to exonerate a doctor who, in attempting to save the life of an expectant mother, finds it necessary to perform an operation that will inevitably result in the death of the fetus. *See also* hierarchicalism.

drugs. Naturally occurring or synthetically manufactured chemicals that, when administered, produce some desired effect on the living being's system. Not included in this nomenclature are substances considered foodstuffs, such as carbohydrates, proteins, lipids and starches. Drugs, when administered under the supervision of appropriate personnel, can be health enhancing (*see also* health care). However, certain classes of drugs can become *habit forming and, when abused, can lead to *addiction or, in large doses, even *death. The abuse of drugs, and the personal and societal hazards inherent in that abuse, is an ethical concern for *society. From a Christian perspective, drug abuse, with its adverse effects on a person's health, also conflicts with the biblical mandate to exercise *stewardship over one's self and with the Pauline injunction against coming under the control of an alien influence rather than being empowered by the Holy Spirit (Eph 5:18).

duty. An action required by either moral or legal *responsibility, or the force inherent in such a responsibility. As a *principle of conduct, the sense of duty demands that the person bound to perform a specific action fulfill that *obligation. Viewed as a motive for conduct, duty is generally understood to be unconditional in nature. If moral agents fail to acknowledge their obligation as bound by duty, they are considered to be morally without excuse.

E

ecology. The study of the environment and the human disposition toward the earth, especially in the sense that it provides the nurturing context for the existence of humans and other living things. The term is derived from the Greek word *oikos,* "house" or "habitat." In the modern era, an understanding of the interrelated character of living species within the context of ecosystems, coupled with the power of technology, has created an awareness of the fragile nature of the earth as the environment for life. Concerns such as pollution, population growth (*see also* population ethics), toxic waste disposal, *biological warfare and the extinction of indigenous species have made ecology one of the leading aspects of applied *ethics today. Although many proponents of ecological concern appeal to non-Christian religious conceptions, Christians have also stood at the forefront of the ecology movement. Christian concern for ecology arises in part out of the biblical teaching regarding human *stewardship over God's creation.

economic system. The way in which a *community or *society organizes itself so as to produce goods and services and make these available to its constituents. Perhaps the two most widely known types of economic systems today are capitalism and *socialism (with communism being a variant of the latter). Ethical issues surrounding economic systems include the means by which a particular system develops and barters its resources; how it utilizes, develops and maintains its work force; and how it integrates with the other systems to benefit the world. Christian ethics has also debated the extent to which a particular economic system, especially capitalism, coheres with Christian principles or reflects Christian values and the Christian understanding of the nature of the *good life. *See also* Marxism.

education, moral. The process of shaping the moral values, beliefs and behaviors of another person or groups of people. At the simplest level, moral education can be an unintentional socialization within a particular context. On the other hand, it can be an intentionally planned educational strategy, designed to shape important dimensions of the *morality of those being educated. The Christian church has tended to integrate moral education with wider aspects of its educating and nurturing role in the lives of its members, especially under the rubric of training in Christian discipleship. Moral education in the church occurs as well in its worship practices. *See also* moral development.

egalitarianism. The belief that all persons have equal political, social and economic *rights regardless of such distinguishing characteristics as sex, ethnicity or even economic status. Egalitarians assert that in some primary sense all humans are equal, despite the fact they are unequal in physical and intellectual capabilities. Some theologians have based the fundamental *equality of all persons on their shared participation in the *image of God. The term is used more narrowly today to refer to the belief that gender is no barrier to leadership roles in the church, but that both women and men may properly be appointed to such positions so long as they are gifted and called by the Spirit to lead the church. *See also* feminist ethics.

ego. *See* id, ego, superego.

emotivism. An alternate term for *noncognitivism, the theory that ethical judgments do not carry cognitive meaning, that is, they do not ascribe moral properties to acts or persons, at least not in any manner that is objectively true or false. Taken to the extreme, emotivism declares that ethical statements are merely the forceful expression of a speaker's emotions. Many proponents, however, add that such expressions have the goal either of commanding a similar emotion in the hearer or of evoking approval or disapproval in the hearer. *See also* prescriptivism.

empirical ethics. The division of philosophical or *general ethics that involves the observation of the moral *decision-making process with the goal of describing or explaining the phenomenon.

employment. A relationship, often voluntary in character, between two parties in which one (e.g., the worker or employee) performs a particular service (e.g., *work) for the other (e.g., the owner, employer or supervisor) in exchange for some other *good, such as financial remuneration. In employment, the employer and employee have certain *duties, *rights and *obligations that govern the relationship. These form the ethical dimension of the relationship. *See also* business ethics; labor ethics; professional ethics.

encyclicals. Originally, a circular letter from a bishop to a church under the bishop's care. The use of the encyclical was later restricted to the leader of the church in Rome. This led to the use of the term in the Roman Catholic Church to refer to the official statements of the pope written to the faithful. The literal name for a papal encyclical is *litterae encyclicae,* and it is used to communicate a wide variety of subjects that concern the church as a whole. Papal encyclicals carry great weight, for they are issued from the head of the church, who as the one deemed to be the vicar of Christ is assumed to write under the authority of Christ himself. Papal encyclicals often touch on or even focus on ethical questions. *See also* canon law.

Epicurus, Epicurean ethics. An ancient Greek philosopher; the ethical system deriving from his school of thought. Epicurus (341-270 B.C.) taught that all knowledge rises from the senses and that the study of *ethics was the highest human occupation. From the ancient Greek thinkers Democritus and Aristippus, Epicurus developed an ethic that espoused the serenity or peace of mind, as opposed to the contemplation of eternal knowledge. He espoused an austere *hedonism, which viewed *pleasure as the sole ultimate *good and pain as the sole *evil. But because pleasure gives way to pain, Epicurus encouraged the avoidance of pleasure as a way of reducing pain, and he espoused *prudence and the value of *friendship as the key to a peaceful, pain-free existence. Later, to be called Epicurean came to be equated with debauchery and self-indulgent *hedonism.

equality. The measure of identical worth and value between two or more entities, especially as applied to human beings. Most philosophical and religious traditions give some place to the idea of equality, and some go so far as to see equality as inalienable. In Christian teaching, the concept of equality is often viewed as connected to the *image of God. It also arises out of the impartiality of God's *love to all humankind, which leads in turn to an ethic that demands that Christians be concerned for the well-being of all persons. *See also* egalitarianism.

eros. A Greek term for *love that prior to New Testament times was used to designate passion, ecstasy and even madness. Hence, *eros* is often used to refer to the impassioned, carnal and irrational. Throughout much of church history, Christian ethicists have debated the value of *eros* as a component of Christian *morality, many thinkers going so far as to view the erotic as too connected to carnal *lust to be of service to the moral life. Today, however, some Christian ethicists are rehabilitating the concept. Some speak about the importance of the erotic within the context of a healthy *marriage, whereas others are developing a wider understanding of the idea that links it with the desire for the other, which in their estimation finds its source in the divine life. *See also* agape.

eschatology, its role in ethics. Eschatology, the Christian teaching regarding last things, has played an important role in *Christian ethics in the modern era. It has been commonplace since the beginning of the twentieth century to assert that Jesus' ethical teachings are only comprehensible when viewed within the apocalyptic understanding of a coming eschatological *kingdom of God. This insight has sparked a debate about the applicability of Jesus' ethic for the present age. More recently the idea has come to the fore that the Christian ethic is related to the eschatological vision of the

Christian *community. According to this view, the Christian community is mandated with the task of living in the present in the light of and as a foretaste of the future eschatological community. As a result, the central *imperative is "become who you will be." This perspective leads to the question of the extent to which life in the eschatological society can form the basis for moral *decision making in the present. *See also* Jesus, ethic of.

ethic of being. The approach to moral reasoning that declares that the ethical task is primarily oriented toward *character and *virtue, or more precisely, the development of what a person ought to be, rather than toward the question of the rightness or wrongness of particular actions. An ethic of being places conduct secondary to character. It gives primacy to judgments of value rather than judgments of moral *obligation. *See also* ethic of doing.

ethic of doing. The approach to moral reasoning that declares that the ethical task is primarily oriented toward the question of the moral status of particular acts. Being concerned above all with the question as to what a person should do, an ethic of doing attempts to construct *standards of conduct, generally by following one of two basic strategies, *deontological ethics or *teleological ethics. The former suggests that the rightness or wrongness of an act is connected to something intrinsic to the act, whereas the latter proposes that such judgments are to be made on the basis of the consequences of a proposed act. *See also* ethic of being.

ethical language. Assertions or expressions that embody ethical perspectives, especially perspectives regarding what is morally *right or *good. Ethicists have differed with each other regarding what ethical language purports to communicate. Some ethicists maintain that ethical language carries cognitive meaning and hence that through such language the speaker is making a specific and perhaps even a certain claim about a particular external state of affairs. At the other end of the spectrum stand those who aver that ethical language carries emotive meaning. Ethical statements are expressions of personal feelings, emotions or attitudes (*emotivism).

ethical egoism. A variety of *teleological ethics or the consequentialist approach to moral *decision making that asserts that each person's sole moral *obligation is to advance the agent's own welfare. Hence, its fundamental maxim states, "Always act in such a manner so as to bring about the greatest amount of *good over *evil for yourself." Or "always act in accordance with your own long-term best interests." The term *egoism* arises from the Greek term *ego,* meaning "I" or the individual self. Some ethicists find the basis for a Christian version of ethical egoism in the biblical injunctions to seek what will be in one's own best interests in the age to come, including participation in eternal life and rewards for service to Christ. Others consider this moral theory to be inimical to the Christian focus on the other evident injunctions to seek the good of others above oneself.

ethics. Moral philosophy, or the division of philosophy that involves the study of how humans ought to live. Ethics focuses on questions of *right and wrong, as well as the determination of the human *good. If *morality involves the actual practice of living out of one's beliefs, then ethics is the study of why these practices are moral or immoral. *Christian ethics, in turn, is the study of how humans ought to live as informed by the Bible and Christian convictions. *See also* medieval ethics.

eudaemonism. An ethical theory that asserts that *happiness is the highest *good and the basis for moral *obligation. *Aristotle is often cited as proposing an ethic of happiness. Yet he understood the term not as denoting a psychological state but as referring to well-being or living well. Christian ethicists debate the question as to whether happiness can form the basis for or the goal of the ethical life, especially in the light of Jesus' admonition to his disciples to seek first the reign and *righteousness of God (Mt 6:33).

eugenics. A movement that encourages the study of heredity or the transference of genetically based traits from one generation of living beings to the next, generally with the goal of improving the hereditary endowment of humankind. Although the idea is as old as *Plato, who toyed with the idea of selective breeding as a means to improve humankind, a movement coalesced in the nineteenth century and influenced *public policy in the twentieth, not only in Nazi Germany, but also in the United States and Canada, both of which allowed the forced *sterilization of certain groups of people and enacted discriminatory immigration procedures. Proponents of the task of improving humankind suggested that this goal was to be advanced in two primary ways: positive eugenics, or the encouraging of healthy, productive and intelligent people to reproduce so as to bring improvement by insuring that superior traits would be passed on to the next generation, and negative eugenics, or the discouraging of parenthood for those who are carriers of "inferior" traits. Eugenics has been deemed ethically questionable on many grounds, including the potential infringement on *human rights it involves, as well as the hubris involved in determining what traits are to be seen as constituting an improved humankind. *See also* genetics, genetic engineering.

euthanasia. The intentional killing, by design or by omission, of a person whose life has been deemed not worth continuing. Although euthanasia was probably used in a variety of circumstances in the ancient Greek and Roman societies, in contemporary Western societies proponents of the practice tend to restrict its potential use to persons who are terminally ill or who are being kept alive by artificial means. In the current debate, ethicists tend to divide the general practice into several varieties. Active euthanasia, or mercy killing, involves the attempt to bring about the death of a person by means of a death-producing agent or procedure, in contrast to passive euthanasia, which entails the intentional avoidance or the discontinuance of steps to prolong life. Voluntary euthanasia is the clinical termination of the life of a patient who, being of sound mind but who has become the victim of debilitating illness or disease, requests that such termination be carried out. *Involuntary euthanasia, in contrast, proceeds without the *informed consent of the patient because he or she is deemed incapable of assisting in the *decision-making process (e.g., as in the case of a comatose person). The ethical character of euthanasia is based on considerations such as the nature of life and *death, the definition of "quality of life" and the attempt to balance personal and societal well-being. *See also* life, quality of; life, right to; life, sanctity of; suicide.

evangelical ethics. The program of engaging in moral reflection by drawing from the theological and moral commitments, together with the vision of reality, that characterize evangelical Christians or the evangelical movement. Evangelicals find the *norm for moral guidance in biblical revelation, as opposed to autonomous human reason, the individual *conscience or *natural law. Furthermore, according to the evangelical vision, the moral life emerges from the transforming work of the Holy Spirit who renews the believer's character through the new birth. This renewal involves the "putting away" of the old way of living and the "putting on" of the new life available through union with Jesus Christ.

evangelism, ethical aspects of. Evangelism is the process whereby the good news of salvation through Christ is communicated to others. Insofar as evangelism is commanded by Christ (Mt 28:19-20), for Christians this task is a moral *imperative. Nevertheless, not all methods of evangelism are ethical. Most Christian ethicists deem unethical such practices as "forced conversion," psychological and emotional manipulation, and the use of financial or other material inducements. Methods are generally judged in accordance with the principle that genuine conversion is voluntary; that is, it is the product of the Holy Spirit's wooing of a person's *will.

evil. The privation or absence of *good; that which opposes, resists or undermines the good; the lack of or that which works against human well-being and the flourishing of creation; the lack of, or that which opposes God's intentions. As these various descriptions suggest, evil can be understood on two levels. It may be viewed as simply a negative state, the lack of the good. It may also be seen as an opposing force, the disposition against or active attempt to thwart the good. The Christian tradition differentiates evil that is connected with the rebellion or fall of moral creatures (humans and angelic beings) from "natural" evils, that is, suffering-producing events that occur through the outworking of the laws of the physical world. The former is explicated in the doctrine of *sin, whereas the latter is sometimes treated within the doctrine of creation or apologetically as part of the wider issue of theodicy (or the problem of evil). *See also* suffering.

existentialist ethics. The approach to *ethics that asserts that ethical reflection finds its genesis in the human condition or in the concrete experience of personal existence rather than in the devising of universally applicable ethical systems. As the designation of a movement in philosophy, existentialism encompasses a wide variety of thinkers in the nineteenth and twentieth centuries, including Søren *Kierkegaard and Jean-Paul Sartre, who, despite the diversity that separates them, all extol subjective individuality in the form of personal involvement in the situations of life as the basis for knowing. Hence, existentialists declare that rather than beginning with some fixed essential nature, humans are "thrown into existence" and create personal meaning through the choices they make. The basis for an existentialist ethic, in turn, is the idea that personal active *decision making, and not the exploration of a theoretical, detached ethical system, is the means to the development of (personal) values and ethical meaning.

experimentation. As the method of inquiry of empirical science, the act or process of examining empirical data and testing hypotheses in order to come to a specific conclusion or result. Experimentation becomes a topic for ethical reflection when the objects of inquiry are living beings (especially humans and animals) and their environments. More specifically, ethicists voice concern about the suffering of test subjects, the environmental impact of experimentation and the future implications of such experiments, especially in the light of such values as *human rights, *animal rights and environmental sustainability (*ecology). *See also* science and ethics.

exploitation. The process by which one party takes unfair advantage of another, usually through manipulation, coercion or deception, in order to accomplish specific ends. Exploitation presupposes universal ethical *standards such as *justice, *fairness and dignity, when defining specific instances of this process. Although it has been a topic of Christian ethical reflection throughout church history, in the modern era the concept of exploitation became a central theme of both Marxist and liberation thought. *See also* liberation ethics; Marxism.

extortion. The act of obtaining something, such as money, from an entity (whether a person, group, corporation or institution) through threats, violence or the misuse of authority. Extortion is generally censured on ethical grounds as a violation of the personhood of the other, and in most Western nations various forms of extortion are illegal.

extrinsic value. *See* intrinsic value.

F

fairness. A *principle of *justice that asserts that all persons in a particular group or all participants in a particular activity ought to contribute to and share in the benefits that accrue to the group in a manner that is equitable when measured according to an assumed or agreed to standard. Although the principle of fairness is universally upheld by ethicists, they sometimes differ as to the standard by which equitable contribution and sharing in the accrued benefits are to be measured. One standard of fairness declares that all participants ought to both contribute equally and receive an equal share of the benefits. The following dictum provides another example: "From each according to his ability, to each according to his needs" (*see also* Marxism; socialism). Finally, some groups follow the principle that a person's share in the accrued benefits ought to be proportionate to his or her contribution. *See also* distributive justice.

faith. A theological term denoting a central aspect of the stance that humans are to have in relationship to God. As the human response to God and God's promises, faith entails both intellectual assent and trust, which results in commitment leading to *obedience. Furthermore, faith and not human effort is the basis for receiving the gift of *righteousness, out of which the moral life flows. Viewed from this perspective, the obedience born from faith—and from the right standing before God that is received by faith—is central to the human moral *imperative. The faith that gives rise to obedience is based on God's own character, especially the divine *faithfulness and trustworthiness, which serves as well as a model for right relationships with God and others. Unbelief, in turn, is often portrayed in the Bible as both the cause of and the root form of rebellion against God. The medieval ethicists, such as *Thomas Aquinas, drew an additional connection between faith and *ethics, for faith was seen as one of the three *theological virtues (alongside hope and *love). In contrast to the four natural virtues (the *cardinal virtues of classical Greek philosophy) to which all persons had a degree of access, the theological virtues were understood to be divine gifts.

faithfulness. A quality of *character that entails remaining steadfast in one's commitment to another person or group of persons, or to one's promises to another person or group, even in the face of adversity, opposition or faithlessness on the part of the other person or group. Such steadfastness, in turn, results in the faithful person being worthy of trust. The biblical narrative recounts the faithfulness of God, which in turn forms the basis for the injunction to God's covenant people to be characterized by faithfulness as well. Viewed from this perspective, human faithfulness is grounded in *faith in God as the faithful one and in God's promises. The result is commitment to God or loyalty to Christ, a stance that is lived out in attitude and conduct and that fosters, by the work of the indwelling Spirit, Christlike *character in the believer resulting in his or her faithfulness in relationships with others. For this reason, Paul lists faithfulness among the fruit of the Spirit (Gal 5:22).

falsehood. A belief, assertion or perhaps even an act that does not accord with truth. Holding to or articulating a falsehood may not necessarily be the result of a deliberate malicious intent. Nevertheless, the term is often used to denote a calculated deception, generally directed toward another person, but sometimes even directed toward oneself (i.e., in the case of people who deliberately deceive themselves). In this sense, a falsehood carries the connotation of being an overt lie. Although propagating a falsehood is generally considered unethical, some ethicists suggest that in a few circumstances such an act could be deemed the lesser of two evils, if not actually morally justifiable. *See also* deontological ethics; honesty; lying.

family. In contemporary Western society, a group of persons forming a household, especially in that they are legally related to each other as spouses and perhaps as parents and children (and possibly including members of the extended group of persons related by blood or legal adoption). In most societies, at least historically, the family has served as the basic unit of *society. In this role, the family has been the context for bearing and caring for children (and possibly subsequent descendants). It has also functioned as a unit within the wider economy of the society. Viewed from the ethical perspective, the family also provides the context for basic moral formation and expression. In the modern era, the nuclear family—consisting of father, mother and children—together with the understanding of *marriage as a covenant between spouses and the context for the *procreation and rearing of children, has provided the most widely held model of family. Today, however, a crucial debate focuses on what precisely constitutes a family, a question that is related to the issue of the proper parameters for the expression of human sexuality. Both marriage and family are used in the Bible as metaphors or pictures of spiritual truths. *See also* cohabitation; common-law marriage.

famine. The condition of an acute and widespread shortage of food. Famines are caused not only by natural disasters such as drought, floods and crop failures, but also by human actions, including *war and the mismanagement of the means of food production. Repeatedly since the time of the early church (e.g., Acts 11:27-30), Christians have been at the forefront of famine relief. *Christian ethics enjoins such actions on the basis of passages in the Bible that present feeding the hungry as a moral *imperative and by appeal to the biblical teaching that universal sharing in "our daily bread" is one of the marks of the *kingdom of God. Some voices, in contrast, have argued against famine relief on the basis of considerations such as the idea—related at least loosely to social Darwinism—that famine is a means by which the human population is regulated (*see also* population ethics). Recently, ethicists have debated the question regarding the extent to which famine in some parts of the world is the product of systemic problems and unjust practices in various parts of the world. Ethical discussions have also considered whether—and how—churches, other groups in *society, corporations or governments might foster systemic changes that would reduce the likelihood of future famines, including a possible global famine. *See also* hunger.

feminist ethics. Ethical reflection or theorizing that locates its basic assumptions in contemporary feminist thought. Feminism is an intellectual movement that opposes *discrimination on the basis of gender and has as its ultimate aim *equality among persons. Feminist theology, in turn, is the attempt to engage in theological reflection on the basis of women's experience or the attempt to set forth theological affirmations that will take seriously the concerns of women, bring to light the experiences of women and foster wholesomeness in women. Feminist ethicists, in turn, begin with women's experience both as a situation out of which ethical concerns are to be raised and as providing a vantage point to set forth an ethical understanding. Although primarily concerned with rectifying unjust treatment of women, feminist ethicists draw from women's experience, myths regarding women, the history of women and the reconstruction of theories about human personhood on the basis of women's vantage point in order to challenge inequalities at all levels of life. Although Christians regard much of radical feminist thought to be beyond the parameters of the traditional Christian faith, some aspects of feminist ethics, especially its critique of injustices in *society, have exposed culturally conditioned shortcomings in Christian thought and have thereby contributed to biblical, theological and ethical reflection. *See also* egalitarianism; liberation ethics.

fetal research, fetal experimentation. Scientific *experimentation on living or dead human fetuses. This research may be directed toward treating a particular fetus who has shown signs of certain genetic disorders or abnormalities, or it may be directed toward the more general goal of advancing medical science, such as by seeking to unlock new techniques for combating diseases or abnormalities. As an ethical question, fetal research is part of a constellation of issues that ranges from *abortion to *eugenics and *genetics (or genetic engineering). Similar to these other dilemmas, fetal research is ethically controversial, in part because of the ongoing debate about the ontological nature, legal standing and hence moral status of the human fetus. Thus, the discussion often centers on the question of the proper balance between the supposed *rights of the fetus and the gain that such research might offer for other persons, for *society as a whole or for future generations of humans. *See also* life, right to; life, sanctity of.

fidelity. *Faithfulness, especially in honoring a commitment, vow or *obligation; loyalty. As a moral category, fidelity is often used with reference to faithfulness to one's *marriage partner, especially in the sexual dimension (*see also* chastity). Fidelity has also been equated with truthfulness.

flesh. The term *flesh* carries a wide variety of meanings, dependent on the context in which it is used. It can refer to the material that makes up physical bodies or to the human body itself. As an ethical concept, it sometimes is used to refer to human existence as embodied creatures with the physical—and, consequently, the moral frailties—involved in this existence. Some ethical traditions assert that the flesh, understood as the physical or embodied aspect of the human person, is the source of moral failure. Paul likewise uses *flesh* as an ethical term and suggests that the flesh is the source of sinful acts, though he does not locate the flesh in the body or physical dimension of the human person. Rather than contrasting flesh with the immaterial, he sees it as the opposite of spirit. Thus, for Paul, *flesh* refers to the human person as a whole being who is susceptible to fall into *sin. *See also* Paul, Pauline ethics.

force. In its most rudimentary form, energy or *power that acts effectively. Force is also the use of physical power or persuasion either to make someone do something or to prevent them from doing something; in other words, to coerce or to constrain. The concept raises the ethical question as to whether the use of force is morally justifiable. Although some ethicists argue that force ought never to be introduced in human relationships, the debate among the majority of thinkers focuses on matters such as the circumstances in which force can be legitimately used, the extent to which force can be administered, and who might justly resort to force.

forgiveness. The process by which a person is released from the consequences of an action against another person or group and restored to a positive relationship to the offended party. Forgiveness is dynamic and multidimensional. Forgiveness from God releases a person from the consequences of *sin and restores a right relationship between that person and God. For this reason, when one person forgives another person, restoration and reconciliation between the parties should likewise follow. Forgiveness is a central aspect of *Christian ethics, connected to other Christian ethical ideals such as *love, mercy and *justice. Moreover, in Christian ethics to forgive—and take steps to be forgiven—is a moral *imperative (Mt 6:14-15).

formalism. The elevation of the outward form to the neglect of the inward substance; the reliance on the outward rituals practiced by a *community with little regard for the values to which the ceremonies are intended to point. Ethical formalism, in turn, views the ethical life as the performance of outward forms, such as *obedience to *laws, legal stipulations and prescribed duties, without giving due heed to the cultivation of proper inner dispositions (*see also* ethic of being; ethic of doing). In the Bible, formalism often takes the form of *legalism, which religious leaders, especially Jesus, condemned.

fornication. Sexual intercourse involving persons who are not married to each other. *Christian ethics condemns both promiscuity and casual sexual relations, that is, relations that lack any formal commitment. Such acts are considered demeaning and depersonalizing. They also violate God's intention for human sexual expression. *See also* adultery; sexuality, sexual ethics.

fortitude. A *virtue, sometimes associated with *courage, that involves the ability to endure misfortune, pain, peril or adversity with steadfast resolve.

free will. The ability, allegedly present in every human person, to act on the basis of one's own rational choice; the ability to choose without constraint or compulsion from among options. The idea of free will is contrasted with *determinism, i.e., the outlook that asserts that an external agent or force determines all human choices. The assertion that each human is endowed with free will is a widely held ethical assumption. As a *principle of *ethics, it suggests that moral actions are not random events, but originate from the volition (*will) and perhaps the *character of the moral agent. Some ethicists argue that free will forms a necessary basis for moral *responsibility.

freedom. The condition of being exempt from or outside the control of another. In Christian thought, freedom is understood as the state of being rescued from the coercive power of *sin in order to be able to live in *obedience to God. In this sense, freedom is connected to the idea of the ability to live in accordance with one's nature or *telos* (goal or purpose) as given by God. In modern Western social and political thought, freedom is used somewhat synonymously with liberty, understood as the right to pursue one's life apart from overbearing governmental restraint or autocratic control. Political theorists also assert that such freedom may be limited or suspended, however, if the governing authorities deem it justifiable and in the best interest of the *society, a caveat that has from time to time been used by dictators to repress freedom and wield *power for political or personal gain. The Western elevation of freedom often leads to a tension between the *good of the society and the *rights of its individual citizens. This introduces one of the ethical issues connected with the term, namely, the question as to the circumstances under which personal freedom ought to give way to the social good. *See also* autonomy.

friendship. The relationship between individuals involving a shared focus on values or common interests. *Aristotle posited three categories of friendship which, in turn, were inherited by the Christian tradition: that based on the *pleasure received from sharing a common activity, that based on the usefulness of the mutual advantage derived from the relationship, and that based on *virtue, which involves loving another because of the moral qualities the other possesses and desiring the *good of that person. The Greek word for friendship used in the New Testament is *philia,* which is sometimes (perhaps erroneously) contrasted with *agapē.* Although many Greek philosophers elevated friendship as an ethical concept, Jesus invested friendship with theological meaning and tied it closely to the self-sacrificial disposition generally connected with *agape (Jn 15:12-15).

G

gambling. A type of transaction between two parties in which something of value is transferred from one to the other solely on the basis of an uncertain outcome of some event or on mere chance. The term is sometimes used in reference to a life decision, but most often it denotes a game in which winners are created at the expense of losers through the wagering of money or valuables. Playing a game of chance for pure amusement is not necessarily considered gambling. Rather, it is the betting—the staking of money on an outcome that is in doubt—that is at the heart of gambling. Gambling raises several ethical issues. Insofar as gambling can develop into a psychological compulsion, it is considered addictive and therefore comes under the moral censure associated with *addictions. Also, gambling comes under ethical scrutiny because of the ramifications of the practice on others, such as family members, the *community in which gambling occurs and *society as a whole. Those who find gambling intrinsically unethical argue that it glorifies chance, undermines the sense of *stewardship, generates profits from the losses of others and appeals to the *vice of covetousness.

general ethics. Synonymous with philosophical ethics, that branch of philosophy concerned with developing a conception of the ethical life in which all humans (or humans in general) could participate and to which all humans could have access through the use of human reason; the branch of philosophy that has as its task the attempt to provide a rational justification for *morality, to which all humans have access, at least in theory, through the innate power of reason. In this aspect, general ethics may be contrasted to religious ethics, which looks to the resources of a particular religious tradition (e.g., *Christian ethics, *evangelical ethics, *Hindu ethics, *Islamic ethics, *Jewish ethics). General or philosophical ethics is often subdivided into the subdisciplines of *empirical ethics, *normative ethics and *analytical ethics.

genetics, genetic engineering. Genetics is the scientific study of genes, chromosomes and genetic variation, especially with a view toward discovering their role in determining the traits that characterize a human person. Genetic engineering is the utilization of the findings of genetics to alter living entities by means of techniques that add genetically determined characteristics to cells that would not otherwise have possessed them. Generally, this involves the production of recombinant DNA (hybrid DNA produced by combining pieces of DNA from different sources). Currently, genetic engineering is used in agriculture as well as in the production of pharmaceuticals and vaccines. The interest in human genetics has resulted in the *Human Genome Project, the attempt to determine the chromosomal location of every human gene, for the purpose of increasing human knowledge as well as eventually curing genetically based diseases. Some ethicists welcome genetics and genetic engineering, because of the potential for *good that the resultant technologies promise. Others argue that any manipulation of the genetic code is in effect "playing God," and can only have disastrous consequences. *See also* eugenics.

genocide. The purposeful attempt to exterminate a specific human social group, such as a religious, ethnic or cultural *community. Genocide has occurred throughout human history, although the term came into common use as a designation of the attempt by Germany under the National Socialist party (1933-1945) to eradicate the Jewish population of Europe (*see* Holocaust). Contemporary Christian ethicists are nearly unanimous in rejecting genocide as unethical, with the possible exception of the practice as commanded by God in the Old Testament era of the conquest of the Promised Land.

gluttony. The excessive or inordinate desire for food and drink, together with the *pleasure that they bring to a person. This type of excessive desire is condemned in the Bible and has been numbered among the *seven deadly sins in Christian tradition.

golden mean. An aphorism coined by *Aristotle that asserts that the excellence of the moral virtues consists in habitual moderation. The *principle of the golden mean suggests that a *virtue lies in the mean between deficiency and excess. Thus, *courage is the mean between cowardice (the *vice of deficiency) and foolhardiness (the vice of excess).

golden rule. A teaching, purportedly found in the sayings of many religious leaders, but given its most widely acknowledged form by Jesus, which declares that people should treat others in the manner in which they would like to be treated (Mt 7:12; Lk 6:31). The negative form of the injunction appears frequently in the literature of antiquity. As an ethical *principle of conduct, the golden rule is the foundational manifestation of the second great commandment, namely, to *love one's neighbor as oneself. The injunction serves to subvert the typical human trait of self-centeredness and refocus one's concern toward the needs of others. *See also* Jesus, ethic of.

good, goodness. In its adjectival form as an ethical term, *good* means, basically, morally excellent. *Goodness,* in turn, means the state or quality of being good. The nature of this moral excellence, however, has been one of the central questions explored by ethicists throughout history. Whereas the focus of the debate in the Greek philosophical tradition has been on the issue of what constitutes a good human, the biblical perspective begins with the moral excellence of God. As a consequence, *Christian ethics does not leave the good at the level of an abstract philosophical concept. Rather, the ground of goodness is the personal God who is active in human history, who enters into covenant with creation, and who is supremely manifested in Jesus Christ. This God is the standard for goodness and determines what is the human good. *See also summum bonum.*

good life. The vision of existence or state of being that a person desires or values most; the ultimate goal toward which a person strives. As an ethical *principle, the good life is foundational to the conception of *morality and the process of ethical *decision making, insofar as most people order their lives ultimately in accordance with what they value supremely.

good works. Conduct or actions that may be deemed *good or morally upright. In Christian thought, such acts are motivated by *love for God and flow out of the desire to obey God's will. They are not intended as means to *merit divine favor or means for personal gain, but are expressions of gratitude to God for the divine unmerited favor already received, and they are an integral part of the life of devotion to God and *imitation of Christ. Finally, good works are not the products of human effort alone, but are the outworking of the indwelling presence of the Holy Spirit. *See also* legalism.

greed. A synonym for *avarice, the excessive and all-consuming desire for material *wealth. According to the Bible, greed is associated with idolatry, insofar as it leads a person to view the accumulation of material possessions, rather than right relationship to God, as the highest *good (the *good life) and it leads a person to trust in personal ability or accumulated treasure rather than in God for one's well-being and security. When it becomes one's central desire, the accumulation of wealth comes to shape both the inner and the social life of the person held captive by greed. For this reason, Jesus taught that a person must eventually choose between serving God and being a slave to the pursuit of wealth (Mt 6:24).

guilt. Guilt can be described either as an objective moral concept or as a subjective feeling. As a moral and legal concept, it refers to culpability; it is the situation of rightly being held responsible before God or some human agency that emerges when a person commits an offense, engages in wrongdoing, transgresses a *law or violates some accepted code of conduct. As a feeling, guilt is a sense of blameworthiness, perhaps coupled with *shame. Guilt as a feeling is linked, at least in theory, to objective guilt, in that guilt feelings ought to arise out of—and only out of—actual objective guilt. One strand of the Christian tradition adds an additional feature: Guilt is also a given condition of fallen humankind. Moreover, the Christian faith declares that because, in Christ, God dealt definitively with human *sin, guilt can be dispelled. This process includes confession, repentance, *restitution and *forgiveness. *See also* original sin.

H

habit. A learned behavioral response to certain stimuli reinforced by repetition. Though some habits may be connected to *instincts, most are acquired. Moreover, habits are generally automatic responses and may at times be compulsive. They mark a specific way a person reacts under particular circumstances. Habits carry moral overtones in that they can be deemed either *good or bad. Both the Greek and the Christian ethical traditions have been concerned with the cultivation of good habits, which are termed *virtues. Some proponents of what may be called the *ethic of being go so far as to suggest that the determination of what habits are virtuous is the chief topic of ethical deliberation, and the formation of such habits is a person's chief ethical task. *See also* custom.

handicapped. A synonym for disabled, the state of being permanently impaired, whether physically or mentally, due to disease, accident, disorder or genetic inheritance, and thereby unable to perform specific functions that those who are not impaired in this manner are normally able to do. The Christian tradition has consistently viewed caring for persons with disabilities as a moral *imperative. Recently, however, ethicists have debated the question of the limits of care in contexts of scarce resources. Also, the question of how quality of life (*see* life, quality of) is to be defined in the case of severely disabled persons has emerged within the wider discussion of *euthanasia.

happiness. Although happiness is generally understood as a psychological state characterized by contentment, as an ethical term it is more often connected to the idea of living well. *Aristotle, for example, described happiness in this manner, and he suggested that it is the goal of life. Ethicists who view happiness as the goal of life generally add that it cannot be attained directly but arises as the byproduct of other pursuits, such as the pursuit of both *virtue and rational activity. Viewed from this perspective, happiness is the sense of peaceful satisfaction connected with the attainment of harmony in life. Some ethicists connect happiness to *pleasure, to which others respond that when pleasure is seen as an end in itself the result is a self-destructive *hedonism that undermines happiness. *See also* eudaemonism.

harm. As a verb, to inflict injury, damage or hurt to a person's physical or mental condition, or a person's reputation; as a noun, that which afflicts a person in such a manner. The moral *imperative to avoid harming another willfully or even unintentionally is codified in the Hippocratic Oath as it is often summarized: "Do no harm."

hate. As a verb, to be strongly averse or hostile toward a person or thing, to regard with intense aversion; as a noun, a set disposition against a person or thing. Often hate is listed as a *vice and is contrasted with *love. Viewed from this perspective, hate quite often finds its expression in violent behavior directed at God or other people. In the Bible, hate also can take on less negative connotations. It can refer to God's set disposition against *sin, or to the relativizing of other loyalties in comparison to a person's primary allegiance as Christ's disciple.

Haustafeln. *See* household codes.

health care. The cluster of programs and services that promote and maintain physical, mental and social well-being. Good health is seen as a positive aim of human beings. In light of that assertion, an aspect of good government is the ability to enable the access of its constituents to quality preventative and curative medical care. The universal right to health care has been the subject of ongoing debate. In the Christian perspective, health care is mandated as a response to *sin and the fallenness of creation. Moreover, good health begins with *shalom* or *peace, and is characterized by a right relationship with God, with others and with creation, and it includes a proper balance among the various aspects of life and existence. *See also* hospice.

hedonism. A widely held theory of value that declares that *pleasure is the highest *intrinsic value. Hedonism asserts that pleasure is always *good for its own sake, whereas pain is always bad, and that pleasure is the only thing that is good for its own sake, whereas pain is the only thing intrinsically bad. Christian ethicists debate whether a Christian hedonism is possible. Some argue that humans are created to enjoy God forever, and therefore the life of devotion to God—rather than the pursuit of worldly pleasures—is the source of highest pleasure. *See also* eudaemonism; Epicurus, Epicurean ethics.

heteronomy. The approach to ethical reflection in which moral and ethical *principles are derived from a source outside the individual, such as revelation or an authoritative institution. Immanuel *Kant rejected heteronomy in favor of *autonomy. In his estimation, morals arise through the exercise of the autonomous rational *will.

hierarchicalism. A theory of *rule-deontologism, also known as graded *absolutism, that declares that actions are to be governed by a multiplicity of rules that form a hierarchy or a scale of priority, with the result that a "lower" rule can be suspended in a situation in which it comes into conflict with a "higher" rule. Critics raise the question as to the difference between suspending a rule and disobeying or violating it. *See also* double effect; prima facie duty.

Hindu ethics. The diverse ethical attitudes that find their source in the attempt to draw out the ethical implications of Hinduism as either a religious tradition or a way of thinking. Because Hinduism is itself a synthesis of a variety of religious and cultural elements and traditions, Hindu ethics is difficult to pinpoint with precision. Nevertheless, the theme of "liberation" is central to Hindu thought, and consequently Hindu ethics is often viewed as seeking to provide a means to liberation. Beginning with the Upanishads (a collection of vedic metaphysical texts that delineate the relationship between humans and the cosmos), Hinduism commonly held that wealth *(artha)*, desire *(karma)* and *duty *(dharma)* are the dimensions of life that, in principle, serve the supreme end of human existence, namely, liberation *(moksa)*. The desire of every Hindu was to reach the goals of wealth, desire and duty, and, once the goals were achieved, to move past them to the fourth ideal, that of the wandering spiritual recluse *(sannyasin)*. The concern of the *sannyasin*, in turn, is the attainment of spiritual knowledge, which lies beyond caste and social *custom.

holiness. A biblical word that refers to the trait connected with the idea of separation from what is common, or even *evil; hence the state of being characterized by purity, wholeness and moral *goodness. God is deemed holy because God is both greater than any of the gods and higher than creation, but also because God is morally pure and perfect, entirely free from *sin, righteous in conduct and steadfast in opposition to sin. When attributed to humans, holiness combines the distinctiveness of being called by God (election) and dedicated to God's purpose (*obedience); hence, it entails being set apart to God for some special purpose. In addition, holiness carries a moral sense, denoting both a heart turned toward God and the resultant way of living that involves both eschewing sin and acting rightly.

Holocaust. The designation of the slaughter of over six million Jews during the period from 1933 to 1945, when the German National Socialist regime sought to eradicate the Jewish people. *See also* genocide.

homicide. The taking of a human life by another human. Homicide can be classified as accidental, culpable or justifiable. *See also* murder.

homosexuality. The condition of or behavioral outworkings of sexual attraction toward a person of the same sex. The term is used in two basic ways: to designate sexual behavior involving persons of the same sex or to denote the psychobiological situation in which a person is erotically aroused exclusively (or perhaps primarily) by persons of the same sex. In traditional Christian thought, homosexual behavior is deemed a deviation from God's intention and therefore sinful. Recently, scientists from various disciplines have debated the question as to whether homosexuality is a static "sexual orientation" and, if so, what its causes might be. This debate has raised a variety of social and legal questions such as how sexual orientation ought to be viewed and what *rights ought to accrue to homosexual persons by virtue of their sexual orientation. It has also triggered a discussion within *Christian ethics as to whether the biblical writers condemn homosexuality as such, or merely a variety of other practices prevalent in ancient societies which involved certain homosexual acts (e.g., idolatry, *pederasty). *See also* bisexuality; lesbian; sodomy; transsexual.

honesty. A *virtue that entails being devoted to truth and truthfulness. As a virtue, honesty gives rise both to pursuing truth (intellectual honesty) and being truthful in relationships with others (moral honesty). *Christian ethics adds an additional dimension, that of "being in the truth," a concept that suggests that honesty can refer to a person's entire existence.

hospice. A program of direct care for terminally ill patients and their families. The term is derived from the Latin word *hospes,* meaning host or guest, and hence originally referred to a place of rest, lodging or shelter for pilgrims or travelers, especially as maintained by a monastic order. Hospice care is intended to relieve patients' pain, help them come to terms with their death and assist them to live as fully as possible in the meantime. It also seeks to help families of patients cope with the illness and with their own bereavement. *See also* hospitality.

hospitality. The practice of taking in strangers, travelers or the sick with the *intention of providing safety, food, shelter and other essentials. Hospitality was understood to be a primary *duty in both the Old and New Testaments, but it has not been emphasized to the same degree in contemporary ethics. *See also* hospice.

household codes *(Haustafeln).* The designation, dating at least to Martin Luther, of the ethical instructions given to classes of persons in first-century households. This form of ethical instruction was used in *Stoic and Hellenistic Jewish circles. They are also found in several New Testament writings (Eph 5:22-6:9; Col 3:18-4:1; 1 Pet 2:18-3:7), where they are structured according to specific paired relationships: husbands-wives, parents-children, masters-slaves. The presence of the household codes in the New Testament raises the question regarding their place in the *Christian ethic. Some ethicists see in these texts direct application to relationships today. Other scholars find no abiding relevance for the household codes, claiming that they reflect a hierarchical pattern of human relationships that is archaic and at odds with the *egalitarianism of contemporary *society and perhaps even of the gospel itself. A third group avers that a close reading of the texts indicates that the household codes actually work to undermine that hierarchical pattern.

Human Genome Project. A joint project, begun in 1990, involving agencies around the world, but coordinated in the United States by the Department of Energy and the National Institutes of Health. The goals of the Human Genome Project are to identify the approximately 30,000 genes in human DNA; to determine their sequences; to store the data and then transfer it to the private sector for development; and finally to address the ethical, legal and social issues that arise from the project. The ultimate intention is to stimulate the development of new medical applications. The project has engendered a lively ethical debate between those who welcome new discoveries, together with the advances in human well-being that they promise, and those who fear that tampering with the DNA sequence entails relegating to humans a role that only God can assume. *See also* bioethics; eugenics; genetics, genetic engineering.

human dignity. The unalterable, inherent value due every person by virtue of being a human being. Although human dignity is a widely recognized concept today, much debate surrounds the basis out of which it arises and its practical implications. In Christian thought, human dignity is often connected to the idea that humans are the *image of God. *See also* equality; human rights.

human nature. The group of qualities that comprise the human essence and hence characterizes each person by virtue of being human. Whether or not there is a human nature has been a topic of philosophical debate, as has been the question as to how such a nature can be discovered. Some propose that the shared human nature consists in the basic physical drives (i.e., *hunger, thirst, safety and sexuality) that humans share with many other creatures, to which must be added the unique features of human existence, such as self-transcendence. Many Christian thinkers aver that the human nature is best understood in the light of the special relationship to God that God wills for humans, as evidenced in the biblical narrative of creation, fall, redemption and new creation. Ethicists are not in agreement regarding the significance for *ethics of positing a human nature. Some argue that the human nature provides a standard for *morality, insofar as our mandate is to actualize our nature, live in accordance with our nature or seek to emulate an ideal human nature. Many Christian ethicists reject any simple appeal to an empirically based understanding of human nature, countering that the fall has distorted God's intention for humankind.

human rights. The set of liberties, claims, powers and immunities possessed equally by all human beings by virtue of their status as humans. Human rights are generally considered unforfeitable and as existing independently of any institution, organization, social structure or government. In fact, human rights are often invoked to constrain actions by institutions or governments as well as by other individuals, and they are often put forth as a standard to which appeal can be directed in the process of judging *laws and policies of institutions and governments. Traditionally, human rights tended to be political in orientation and to define liberties deemed to be possessed by all persons. More recently, some theorists have expanded the idea to include social and economic aspects of life, such as the right to an adequate standard of living. A crucial issue that separates many within *Christian ethics from their counterparts in the philosophical tradition is that of the source of such *rights. Whereas the approach followed in *general ethics tends to view rights as intrinsic to the human person or as derived from some type of *natural law, Christian theorists are likely to appeal to God and God's relationship to humankind for the basis of the idea of *natural rights that they might propose.

humanism. The philosophical perspective that exalts the value and dignity of human persons (*see also* human dignity; human rights), and as a result has as its goal the improvement of the human condition. In the modern era, humanism has often come to be set in contrast to Christianity and to represent the rejection of tradition and revelation in favor of human reason. This secular humanism has tended to deny the reality of the supernatural and to elevate the rational and cultural accomplishments of humankind. It has also tended to posit an anthropocentric universe, in contrast to the theocentric perspective espoused by Christians. Despite such differences, to some extent humanism is dependent historically on the Christian elevation of humankind and the human person, especially as these themes emerged in the Renaissance.

humanitarianism. A personal disposition that desires, or a broad social movement that seeks, the betterment of the living conditions of humankind, but particularly of the marginalized, disadvantaged or downtrodden. As the commitment to improving the lives of others, humanitarianism is based on a sense of *compassion for persons who are either in need or have been denied the opportunity to reach their potential. Although the humanitarian impulse is found in many religious and philosophical traditions, it is sometimes viewed as endemic to the Christian faith because of the Christian emphasis on *love for neighbor. *See also* beneficence; benevolence.

hunger. The need or craving for food; as an ethical term, the chronic lack of nourishment experienced by particular persons or people groups, especially as it results in starvation. Hunger takes on ethical connotations, in that it occurs in a world where global food supplies are typically plentiful, and thus where some peoples enjoy abundance while others are wanting. Since the rise of awareness of and concern for world hunger in the 1960s, ethicists in the West have debated various questions regarding the causes of and proper ethical response to this phenomenon. The Christian tradition views providing food for the poor and needy as a moral *imperative. *See also* famine.

hypocrisy. The act of pretending to be what one is not. *Hypocrisy* originated as a technical term in Greek drama that meant playing a part by an actor who in actuality bears no relation to the role itself. In the Bible, Jesus condemned hypocrisy as the feigned façade of goodness that a person uses to cover his or her true self-interested motives (Mt 6:1-5; 7:3-5).

I

id, ego, superego. The abstract concepts that represent the components or divisions of the tripartite personality as outlined in the psychological structural theory of Sigmund Freud. In Freud's scheme, the id is the basic level of psychic organization. It contains the instinctual drives concerned with sex, *hunger and safety (*see also* instincts). The ego is the level of psychic organization responsible for perception, memory, reason and judgment. The ego develops from the id, and seeks to modify or control the basic impulses of the id. The superego, in turn, represents the prohibitions or moral demands that a person has derived from authorities such as parents and teachers, and it influences the ego on the unconscious level. In Freud's assessment, the conflict between the id and the ego is understood to be the primary source for neuroses.

idealism. As a nontechnical term, the pursuit of excellence or the ideal, as opposed to goals deemed more realistic or modest. As a philosophical term, the system of thought that asserts that reality is ultimately mental or spiritual in nature rather than physical or material, and that the latter is derived from mind. It can also refer to the belief that the only reality we can know or conceive of is ultimately mental or spiritual. Idealist ethics, in turn, identifies moral *obligation with some sort of universal will, *duty, *categorical imperative or absolute spirit. It assumes that ethical values find their source in some ultimate spiritual reality, that humans can come to know universal moral *principles (*see also* universal moral judgments), and that humans possess the *freedom to obey the moral principles they discover. Gottfried Leibniz may have been the first to use the term in its philosophical sense. He was followed in this, albeit with variations in usage, by George Berkeley, Immanuel *Kant, Johann Fichte, Georg Hegel (whose name is most often associated with idealism) and Josiah Royce. As an ethical theory, idealism has been supplanted by *utilitarianism and, more recently, *relativism, which in varying ways all ground moral judgments in the material dimension.

illegitimacy. With reference to assertions or patterns of reasoning: illogical, unsound or contrary to what is actually the case; not worthy of further consideration. With reference to personal parentage: born out of wedlock, or being the child of a woman and a man who are not spouses to each other. Illegitimacy once carried grave social stigma and even loss of inheritance *rights. This is evident, for example, in the charge of illegitimacy that Jesus' opponents hurled at him. Caring for persons who have suffered the ill effects of illegitimate birth could be seen as a part of the biblical injunction to minister to widows, orphans and aliens. In Western societies, the sting of "irregular" parentage has largely disappeared.

image of God *(imago Dei)*. A biblical term that denotes the special place of humankind in creation and as a consequence has served as a central concept in the Christian understanding of the human person. Various proposals have been put forth as to the exact nature of the *imago Dei,* the most widely held being that the term denotes a particular power or ability, such as reason or volition, that is present in each person by virtue of being created by God and which may be found in God in a primary manner. In the Genesis creation account, in contrast, the concept seems to refer to the human vocation to be God's representative within creation. In *ethics, the assertion that humans are the *imago Dei* has been used as the basis for asserting the eternal value of the individual, and by extension as providing a foundation for *human dignity and *human rights or for arguments relating to several ethical questions, ranging from *abortion and *euthanasia to *genetics and genetic engineering.

imitation of Christ *(imitatio Christi).* As an ethical concept, an approach to the ethical life that considers the pathway to moral living to consist in discipleship or following after Jesus. The idea is often seen as originating from Jesus himself, for he not only called others to be his disciples, he instructed them to follow him and, above all, to *love each other after the pattern of his love for them (Jn 13:34; 15:12). The term inspired the title for the popular medieval devotional treatise written by Thomas à Kempis. More recently, the idea of imitating Christ has taken the form of asking in every situation—in keeping with the theme of the popular nineteenth century novel by Charles Sheldon, *In His Steps*—the question, What would Jesus do? Although the *imitatio Christi* remains a widely held theme of *Christian ethics, many ethicists would aver that it cannot be reduced to any single simple formula. *See also* imitation, ethic of; Jesus, ethic of.

imitation, ethic of. In general, any ethical proposal that has at its core the idea that the ethical life finds its ultimate source in the example of another. One variety is closely linked to the concept of discipleship and thereby is an outworking of the principle that disciples are to imitate their master. In this sense, a Christian ethic of imitation closely coheres with the idea of the *imitation of Christ. Throughout his ministry, Jesus pointed to his own example as the pattern for ethical living. Yet the Christian ethic of imitation goes further. Jesus is not merely a great hero to be emulated. Instead, the disciple is the recipient of the *love of the Master, and as a result the Christian ethic of imitation entails the devotion, the loving response, of the disciple to the Master. Finally, insofar as Jesus also pointed his disciples to the example of God, the Christian ethic of imitation looks to God and the narrative of God's relationship to creation as the ultimate transcendent foundation for ethical concepts and values and for the moral vision of the Christian *community. *See also* Jesus, ethic of.

immorality. As a general term, any conduct that transgresses moral prohibitions, conflicts with moral *principles or violates proper moral sensitivities (*see* morality, morals). More specifically, immorality regards *standards of sexual morality (*see* sexuality, sexual ethics) and hence denotes the violation of sexual mores.

imperative. As an ethical term, an injunction that defines what is deemed *right or morally obligatory; an action that is considered to carry moral necessity. Immanuel *Kant distinguished between hypothetical and categorical imperatives. A hypothetical imperative is a command issued with a view toward a particular goal or end, whereas a *categorical imperative commands an act that is inherently *good. Kant believed that only the categorical imperative held the status of a moral imperative.

in vitro fertilization. Literally, fertilization "in glass," thus, a reproductive procedure wherein a human egg is inseminated outside the body in a laboratory setting and then implanted in the womb of either the genetic mother or a surrogate. This technique of conception opens the possibility for persons not related to the intended mother or father of the child to donate either the egg or the sperm or both. In vitro fertilization is often hailed as providing a way for persons to become parents who would otherwise be hindered by their physical condition. Nevertheless, some ethicists find the procedure problematic, insofar as it makes possible the inclusion of a third party into the reproductive process and thereby potentially violates the exclusivity of the marital bond. *See also* procreation; reproductive technologies; test tube babies; zygote.

incest. Sexual contact between persons of close kinship, including a stepparent and a stepchild. The prohibition against sexual relations involving close blood relatives arises in part because children born from such liaisons face increased risk of genetic disorders. Whatever the context, incest often causes severe psychological trauma.

individualism. An approach to social and ethical theory that suggests that the locus of decision and action lies in the individual human person and that people derive their personal identities from the choices that they make as individuals, more than from the groups or communities in which they participate (*see also* collectivism). Modern individualism has its roots in the Renaissance, which elevated the place of humans in the cosmos; the Reformation, which viewed salvation as personally experienced together with the concept of direct access of each person to God; and the Enlightenment, which elevated autonomous reason, individual *rights and the pursuit of personal *happiness, as well as the idea that *society is a conglomerate of individuals knitted together by a social contract. *See also* autonomy.

industrial ethics. The intellectual endeavor that seeks to apply ethical *principles to questions associated with industrialization and industrial societies. Examples of the issues pursued include fair labor practices, technological advancement, the *rights and well-being of consumers and the environmental impact of industrial activities. In issues such as these, the debate often focuses on the balance among the interests of the firm, the workers and the public or *community at large. *See also* business ethics; labor ethics.

inequality. The condition of being unequal. Although a situation of inequality is not necessarily morally suspect, it becomes so when inequality is perpetrated in a situation that rightfully ought to be characterized by *equality.

infanticide. The killing of an infant either by the parents or with their express permission. Although infanticide was a common practice in the ancient Mediterranean world, it fell out of favor, largely due to the influence of Christianity. Ethicists today are in general agreement that infanticide motivated by *malice is unethical. More controversial are those cases of infanticide that stem from an attempt to extend mercy to a child suffering extreme pain or a low quality of life (*see* life, quality of) because of some infirmity or physical or mental disorder. *See also* euthanasia.

informed consent. The act of agreement on the part of an individual to a procedure that is understood to be so far-reaching in its potential consequences that the inclusion of the individual is mandated. Informed *consent requires that the person be given appropriate and adequate information as to the nature, benefits and possible risks involved with the procedure. Informed consent has been an important consideration in the discussion of such life-and-death issues as *euthanasia.

innocence. The quality or condition of being deemed free from *evil, complicity or *guilt. The concept of innocence is important in many areas of *ethics. For example, the *just war theory argues that noncombatants are to be viewed as innocent and therefore cannot be the target of military action in any *war that is truly just.

instincts. A predisposition to behave or act in a certain way, without any previous foresight or knowledge of the behavior or act. Instincts are generally distinguished from *habits in that the former are believed to be innate, rather than the product of either repeated action or social conditioning. Freud contended that instincts were stimuli arising from within the person, and he conceived them to arise from the *id and hence to be connected to biological needs.

institutional ethics. Institutions are social organizations established to meet specific human needs or to reflect specific human values. An institution may take a range of forms including that of a *family, a school, a church or an army. Institutional ethics, in turn, is the exploration of the normative understandings of how institutions are structured and managed.

integrity. As a general concept, the quality or state of being whole or complete. As an ethical term, uprightness in *character, authenticity; the situation in which outward conduct arises out of and coheres with sound, inwardly held moral *principles. To act in accordance with such principles is to act with integrity. The Christian vision of integrity suggests that personal authenticity entails living in accordance with moral principles arising out of God's intention for human existence, or acting in accordance with personal convictions that are based on an understanding of God's purposes for creation, humankind and the person as a disciple of Jesus.

intention. The motive that dictates a specific action. An intention may take the form of the desire for a specific result, which may be within a person's *power to effect. Intention in cases of criminal behavior is generally seen as pivotal in determining the *guilt of the accused. Many ethicists argue that intention must be invoked in the task of determining the positive value of specific acts, whereas others aver that an act that has a good result is *good, regardless of the intention of the actor.

international order, internationalism. International order is the designation for a purported specific manner in which, or specific system of *principles in accordance with which, nations either naturally relate or ought to relate to one another. Some theorists maintain that national sovereignty is the fundamental organizing principle of international order, whereas others advocate the ceding of sovereignty to some type of global institution or tribunal. A third perspective appeals to the supposed common set of *norms and *standards that, because they are connected to *human nature, are common to all humans regardless of nationality; these principles, in turn, ought to govern international relations. Christians posit an international order when they set forth the theological assertion of the universal rule of God. Internationalism is the understanding of international order that asserts that political and economic cooperation among nations is the best means toward the *good of all.

intrinsic value. Intrinsic value and extrinsic value, distinction between which dates at least to *Aristotle, denote differing bases whereby humans value and disvalue. Something is said to have intrinsic value when the ground of its value is perceived to lie within its own nature, that is, when it is valued for itself rather than for its effects. In contrast, something has extrinsic value when the ground of its value lies in its relationship to another value, that is, when it is valued for its effects. For example, some would argue that *pleasure is an intrinsic value, in that it is valued for itself (*hedonism). Owning an automobile, in contrast, is an extrinsic value; it is valued for its results, including ease of getting from place to place, but perhaps ultimately because it brings pleasure. Viewed from this perspective, judgments about extrinsic value are based on judgments about intrinsic value.

intuition. A means to knowledge that appeals to an immediate insight into a particular reality or state of affairs that arises apart from inference or general rules. *Kant understood intuition to be the passive sense-awareness that produces a specific information base through the cooperation of imagination and discursive understanding; this intuited knowledge yields a type of data whose detail was the responsibility of the sciences to establish. *See also* intuitionism; prima facie duty.

intuitionism. Also known as nonnaturalism, a theory of justification that asserts that basic ethical concepts are gained through *intuition rather than deduced from sense perception or scientific observation. Because these concepts arise through intuition, rather than by deductive reasoning, they are self-evident. According to G. E. Moore, goodness (*see* good, goodness) is the best example of an ethical concept that is self-evident and known through direct apprehension. Ethical judgments, statements about what is *right, in turn, are derived from this direct perception of goodness, for *right* means "cause of a good result." *See also* justification, moral.

involuntary. An adjective used to denote an action that is coerced; an action that does not arise out of the actor's personal choice or *free will. In contemporary ethics, the term is used with respect to confinement or hospitalization due to criminal activity or mental illness or, in contrast to voluntary *euthanasia, to denote a situation in which death is hastened by means of actions that proceed without the *informed consent of the patient.

Islamic ethics. Moral reflection that appeals to or is derived from Islamic religious documents and traditions, including the Qur'an, the *hadith* or traditions of Muhammad, and the *shariʿa* or religious law. The emphasis of Islam is on conformity or *obedience to the *law. In Islamic ethics, an action is either commanded or forbidden by God, as opposed to simply being *right or wrong.

J

Jesus, ethic of. The ethic of Jesus is primarily encapsulated in the first three books of the New Testament and expounded by the New Testament writers. Jesus' ethic arose out of his proclamation of the eschatological *kingdom of God, which called kingdom citizens to obey the king and to *love each other. According to Jesus, inward piety, rather than outward conformity to the *law, marks true *obedience to God, a piety precipitated by a radical transformation that leads to a willing obedience to God. Furthermore, Jesus proposed a twofold ethic of imitation and devotion. Jesus enjoined his disciples to follow his example. Such imitation, however, was to be motivated by a devotion to Christ that fosters an increasing conformity to Jesus as their Lord. *See also* eschatology, its role in ethics; imitation of Christ; New Testament ethics; Sermon on the Mount.

Jewish ethics. The Jewish approach to *ethics is inextricable from Jewish religion, which appeals to sources such as the Torah, Mishnah, Talmud, midrashim and other religious works. The basic premise of Jewish ethics is that God is holy and God's people are to be holy as well (*see also* holiness). The result is an understanding that links worship to a way of living, which might be characterized as encompassing personal and social *righteousness. The Jewish vision came to view the moral life as a kind of perfection and the pathway to perfection as adherence to the revealed law of God, an adherence, however, that included the concept of *love for God and others. Although broad in scope, in that it brings into its purview the totality of human life, the Jewish teachers did not consider the Jewish ethic to be universal in application, but incumbent only on members of the Jewish community, insofar as they alone owe God *holiness as God's covenant partners. *See also* Old Testament ethics.

judgments, types of. Some ethicists divide the various judgments humans make into four basic types. Judgment of moral *obligation state what a person is morally obligated to do or be, whether directed to a specific individual in a specific situation or encompassing a broad range of persons and situations (e.g., people ought to tell the truth). Judgments of nonmoral obligation offer injunctions, but the violation of these is not deemed to be morally culpable (e.g., on fourth down and thirty, a football team ought to kick). Judgments of moral value express what is, or ought to be, valued, and can take the form of a particular or a general statement of value (e.g., my father was a good man). Finally, judgments of nonmoral value express values that are not moral in nature (e.g., don't wear that shirt; it's just not your style). *See also* value judgments.

just war theory. A moral perspective on *war that delineates the criteria under which such combat can be deemed ethically justified or justifiable. Although Cicero may have been the first thinker to articulate a thoroughgoing theory, the Christian attempt to grapple with this idea finds its beginnings in the thought of *Augustine. During the barbarian invasion of the Roman Empire, Augustine suggested that even though no war is ever fully just, the reluctant and restricted use of *force by Christians might be necessary when charitably defending a neighbor from an assailant, such as the foreign army's attack on Rome. In the wake of Augustine, Christian thinkers devised various versions of the theory. A war is generally considered just if and only if it is waged for a just cause, is motivated by a just *intention, comes as the last resort, is pursued by a legitimate governmental authority, has limited ends in view, exempts noncombatants from attack and carries a reasonable hope of success. In the modern age, the debate over just war theory has intensified as weapons of mass destruction made it increasingly difficult to differentiate between combatants and noncombatants, as well as to wage war with reasonable hope of success. *See also* biological warfare.

justice. A *virtue characterized by the rendering of what is due or merited, *fairness and impartiality. According to *Plato, who typifies the approach of Greek philosophical or *general ethics, justice is the integrative *cardinal virtue, for it involves the harmonious functioning of *wisdom, *courage and *temperance, as ordered and ruled by reason. The Christian understanding finds its basis in divine justice. Rather than showing favoritism, God treats all persons fairly and impartially. Divine justice means that God cares for all persons, including the unrighteous (Mt 5:45) and intends salvation for all, regardless of ethnicity or other human distinctions (Acts 10:34-35; Gal 3:28-29). Divine justice also entails *compassion, especially for the less fortunate (Ps 146:7-8). In the tradition of *Christian ethics, justice came to be viewed as a virtue that flows from and is tempered by *faith, hope and *love. Philosophical discussions of justice generally divide the concept into three forms: *distributive justice (the fair distribution of goods and services, as well as the fair sharing of responsibilities among participants in a *community), *remedial justice (the correction of past unjust distributions) and retributive justice (the restoration of a right that has been violated or making recompense for that violation; *see also* restitution, retribution).

justification, moral. Although moral justification is often understood as the offering of a defense by appeal to a reason or reasons for an action that has been perceived as possibly being wrong, immoral or unethical, as an ethical term it carries the more general sense of supplying an adequate rationale for moral choices or moral assertions. In its more technical sense, moral justification refers to the task, explored under the discipline of *analytical ethics, of exploring the basis for ethical judgments (*see also* judgments, types of). The three most widely held theories of moral justification are *naturalism, *intuitionism and *noncognitivism. *See also* metaphysical moralism.

juvenile ethics. Juvenile ethics particularly designates the manner in which criminal law deals with juvenile offenders. Most industrial societies have established an age at which juveniles or minors become criminally responsible for their behavior. Prior to attaining this age, a special justice system usually deals with juvenile offenders. At the heart of juvenile ethics is the presupposition that juveniles are in the maturation process and that their delinquency at a young age will eventually mature into responsible law-abiding behavior as an adult.

K

Kant, Immanuel (1724-1804). One of the leading philosophers of the Western tradition. Kant's thought, which grew out of and formed a response to the Enlightenment, especially its emphasis on the primacy of reason in human life and in the pursuit of knowledge, has had a profound affect on subsequent philosophy, theology and *ethics. Kant's *Groundwork of the Metaphysic on Morals* (1785) is his best known work on ethics and reflects his belief that ethics is characterized by an a priori quality, that is, that the moral law cannot be deduced from experience. At the heart of his proposal is the idea that conduct is to be governed by a moral law, to which each person, as a rational and free individual, would both affirm and establish as a universal precept. Kant denoted this moral law the *categorical imperative. In so doing, he elevated the idea of the good will, which he understood as the *will to do one's *duty simply because it is one's duty.

Kierkegaard, Søren (1813-1855). A nineteenth-century Danish philosopher and Christian thinker, who gained widespread influence in the twentieth century, especially insofar as he is sometimes hailed as being the father of existentialism (*see also* existentialist ethics). The most cited themes of his writings include his emphasis on the subjective nature of truth and his elevation of concrete existence rather than universal *principles as the locus of *ethics. Kierkegaard divides the moral pathway into three stages: the aesthetic, the ethical and the religious. People begin at the aesthetic stage, which consists in the pursuit of *pleasure. The ethical stage is characterized by a sense of decisiveness, narrative continuity and personal depth that the aesthetic stage lacks. The ethical, in turn, leads to the religious stage. Kierkegaard contrasted the attempt to base one's life on *obedience to the moral strictures codified as ethical universals with the life of *faith, in which a person stands before God and seeks to obey God in each concrete situation.

kingdom of God. God's kingly reign, God's action in asserting rightful sovereignty over creation. Viewed from the perspective of the New Testament, the divine rule was not only the central message of Jesus, but was actually inaugurated in his life, ministry, death and resurrection, and the subsequent outpouring of the Holy Spirit in the world. In one sense, the kingdom of God has arrived, for Christ is reigning now. At the same time, the church—which bears witness to the kingdom and is not to be simply equated with it—awaits the future consummation of the divine reign. This "already, but not yet" character of the kingdom of God forms the background for and introduces a unique creative tension into *Christian ethics. The expectation of the future kingdom of God provides Christian ethics with its central vision. Christians are mandated to seek the implementation of the ethical goals of the kingdom of God. At the same time, Christians realize that these goals will never be attained completely until the kingdom comes in its fullness. *See also* eschatology, its role in ethics.

koinonia. A Greek word used in the New Testament to denote fellowship, communion and, in a limited sense, *community. The basic idea of New Testament *koinonia* is participation in what is held in common, being conscious of belonging to one another as those who form a unique community and consequently sharing with one another. The sense of *koinonia* among Christians is driven by devotion to Christ, as well as a realization of a common status as those who by the Holy Spirit have been placed in Christ and therefore belong to God. *Koinonia,* therefore, refers both to a shared sense of identity and a moral *imperative to act toward one another in a manner befitting those who participate together in the one fellowship of Christ.

L

labor ethics. The discipline of ethical study that analyzes the moral dimensions of the relationship between labor and management. Labor ethics is especially concerned with the moral questions that arise out of that relationship, such as substandard wages or hazardous work environments. *See also* business ethics; employment; industrial ethics.

laissez faire. A phrase first used by French writers in the eighteenth century meaning "let do." In contemporary usage it refers to the theory of political economics that asserts that government should follow a policy of limited interference in the activities of individual businesses. *See also* business ethics; economic system.

law. The sum total of rules of conduct established by a particular authority viewed as a whole; any one of these rules of conduct; the condition in which rules of conduct are enforced, as in the phrase, "law and order" or the "rule of law." Ethicists are in agreement that law is necessary for the common welfare of *society. The particular laws encoded and enforced by the Roman Catholic Church are known as *canon law. In the Christian tradition, law is seen as having its ultimate source in God, who as the sovereign creator has the prerogative of determining how humans ought to live and of demanding that humans live in accordance with the divine design. Beginning in the Old Testament, the Bible develops the idea of law. Yet it does not begin this development from a conception of God as an austere lawgiver, but as the covenant partner of Israel (and by extension of all humankind). The (Mosaic) law, in turn, codifies what it means to be God's covenant partner. The New Testament views the law of Moses, which cannot bring about human *righteousness before God, as fulfilled in Jesus Christ on behalf of those who as a result of his work are partners with God in a new covenant. On this basis, Christian ethicists understand the law as having three uses. *See also* law, uses of; natural law.

law, uses of. According to Christian teaching, the *law—especially, the Mosaic law—which finds its source in God, has not been eradicated, even though it has been fulfilled in Christ. The law continues to function in the world, in the sinner and in the believer in two or perhaps three ways. Luther spoke of two uses of the law. First, the law fulfills a general use, in that it acts as God's gracious restraint on *sin, as human government "bears the sword" (Rom 13:4) so that through the rule of law humans might not become as sinful as they otherwise would be. Second, in its theological or salvific use, the law serves as the prelude to the gospel, for by pointing out how we ought to live, it indicates our sinfulness, so that we might come to God for divine grace, mercy and *forgiveness. To these two uses, some Reformers, including Calvin, added a third. The law instructs believers about God's will for holy living. The third use of the law opened the way for the Reformed concept of *sanctification as growth in *obedience to God's will as set forth in the precepts of the Bible. *See also* Reformation ethics.

legalism. The conception of *ethics that identifies *morality with the strict observance of *laws or that views adherence to moral codes as defining the boundaries of a *community. Religious legalism focuses on *obedience to laws or moral codes based on the assumption that such obedience is a means of gaining divine favor. *See also* formalism; good works.

lesbian. A female homosexual, that is, a woman who is erotically aroused primarily if not exclusively by females or who engages in sexual acts with females. The term is derived from the Greek island of Lesbos, the home of the female poet Sappho, who was said to have encouraged young women of the island to develop erotic relationships with each other as part of the worship of Aphrodite. In recent years, the term has taken on a political and social tone as well. Some women call themselves lesbians not so much to denote their sexual preference as to assert in a poignant manner their radical rejection of patriarchy. *See also* homosexuality.

libel. *See* slander.

liberalism, ethical. A theory of *social ethics that asserts that the positive aspirations shared by all humans can provide the basis for the construction of *society; a theory of *personal ethics that elevates the moral reasoning abilities of the individual as the locus of ethical *decision making.

liberation ethics. An approach to *ethics closely connected to liberation theology, which draws from the biblical theme of liberation and is seen as providing the basis for a concern for the poor, the marginalized and the oppressed. The genesis of liberation theology lies in the work of several Latin American Roman Catholic theologians, including Gustavo Gutiérrez, in the late 1960s and the 1970s. In a situation in which people were being victimized by "institutionalized violence," Gutiérrez called on the church to cast its lot with the oppressed because God had likewise done so, as is borne out in the biblical narratives of liberation. The church is to work for social transformation because in so doing it joins God's cause in the world. Since the 1970s, the theme of liberation has broadened to encompass the concerns of various marginalized peoples in the world, as well as in North America: African Americans, Hispanics, Native Americans, Asian Americans and women. In addition, recent years have witnessed a growing convergence between liberation ethics and the work of activists in a variety of areas, including *feminist ethics, *ecology and *animal rights. *See also* praxis.

libertarianism. As a metaphysical concept, the view that rejects *determinism in favor of *free will, and hence maintains that people are responsible for the moral choices they make insofar as these choices are not determined by antecedent circumstances. As a political concept, the view that elevates individual *rights rather than the prerogatives of the state or other corporate entities. Political libertarianism, which finds its genesis in the classical liberalism of John Locke, acknowledges that coercive institutions, such as government, are necessary and thus are justified insofar as they promote liberty, but adds that such institutions ought to confine their coercive role to that of preventing people from engaging in wrongful acts of commission.

life, quality of. A term used in various ethical debates, but especially in the debate about *euthanasia, to suggest that for a meaningful existence a person must not only be physically alive but also be able to experience to at least a limited degree the various qualities that constitute human life as unique or that belong to the essence of being human (*see also* human nature). Quality of life considerations are generally invoked in situations in which a person or group of people, such as the elderly or the severely medically disabled, are enjoying only a limited qualitative existence in comparison to what would be considered normal living. The term is especially used in discussions surrounding medical cases in which the prolongation of physical life would not only severely affect the future quality of life of the persons involved, but are deemed to have ethical implications as well, such as persons diagnosed with birth defects and the terminally ill. Opponents of appeals to quality of life point out that no standard description of what factors constitute meaningful human existence has gained universal agreement. *See also* life, sanctity of.

life, right to. The assertion that every human being has a fundamental right to live, and perhaps that this right forms the basis for all other *human rights. *Christian ethics often appeals to the concept of the *image of God as the basis of the right to life. The *principle of the right to life has been used as an argument against *abortion and to a lesser extent *euthanasia. Often at issue in debates about the right to life is not so much whether each person has such a right, but at what stage in the developing fetus a human being with *rights is present. Also, some ethicists would deny that the right to life is inviolate or that it necessarily overrules all other considerations in every situation. *See also* life, sanctity of.

life, sanctity of. The belief that human life is unique and hence sacred. The *principle of the sanctity of life is often seen as demanding that a human being always be treated with respect and especially that a person's life not be ended prematurely, unduly, carelessly or merely for reasons of utility. In *Christian ethics, the sanctity of life refers to the particular respect that ought to be given to human life because it is both a gift from God and it comes ultimately under God's sovereignty. In this theological perspective each human being is considered to be incalculably precious to God and created for an eternal *telos*. The sanctity of life is often invoked as providing the foundation for the existence of a supposed right to life (*see* life, right to), which forms in turn the basis of all other *human rights. The sanctity of life has been invoked in a range of issues, including *abortion, *homicide, *cloning, *capital punishment, *war and *euthanasia.

living will. A document that stipulates the desires of an individual regarding possible treatment during a terminal illness, especially in the event that the individual becomes incompetent to make a decision. Usually, a living will addresses the circumstances under which resuscitation ought or ought not to be attempted, but it sometimes includes matters relating to the use of life-support systems as well.

love. A central *virtue in most ethical traditions, one that denotes an attitude toward another involving both an affection for and a deep commitment to the other. In the Christian tradition, love (especially *agape) is an expression of the essential nature of God, the central characterization of the relationship between God and humans, and the chief virtue that is to characterize Christians in their relationships to God and one another, as shaped by the indwelling Holy Spirit. The connection between love and God's own character gives rise to the Christian focus on love as the fundamental characteristic of Christian discipleship and hence of *Christian ethics. Many Christian thinkers suggest that the essence of love is unconditional giving of oneself for the sake of others. *See also* theological virtues.

lust. An intense or even excessive desire or craving. Although the pursuit of sexual *pleasure is often equated with lust, the meaning of the term is not limited to this dimension. In *Christian ethics, lust is numbered among the *seven deadly sins.

lying. The telling of a *falsehood, or a concealment of truth with the *intention of deception. In that truth is an aspect of God's character, to lie is to act against godly *character. Lying likewise undermines the veracity of relationships and hence the fabric of *community. Although truth-telling is almost universally acknowledged as a moral *imperative, ethicists have debated the conditions under which either withholding the truth or actually telling a falsehood becomes the lesser of two evils.

M

magisterium. The group of persons, generally vocational theologians and church officials, who by virtue of their place within the teaching office of the Roman Catholic Church possess the authority to determine the content of and to pass on to others official church doctrine, teachings and practices. The *Magisterium* in a narrow sense designates the authoritative body of teachings within the Roman Catholic Church, as set forth by the bishops acting under the authority of the pope. The teaching of faith and morals is the primary objective of the magisterium.

malice. A disposition consisting of the desire to inflict injury or *suffering on another person. Malice may take the form of simply gloating over another's misfortune, or it can come to be expressed as an actual act of violence directed against the other person.

Manichaean ethics. An ethical system based on the ontological dualism of or akin to Manichaeism. Manichaeism is a system of religious and philosophical thought that originated in the teachings of the Iranian prophet Mani. Manichaeism propagates a dualistic cosmology that asserts a primal conflict between the principles of light and darkness. Manichaean ethics, in turn, is characterized by an emphasis on purity and on the otherworldly origin of evil. Manichaeans renounced the material and physical in order to maintain the purity needed to pass into the realm of light after *death. Because of its radical ontological dualism between *good and *evil, Manichaeism tended to exonerate the individual from personal *responsibility for evil.

marriage. The voluntary and exclusive union of a man and woman into a social and sexual bond that is intended to be lifelong and is to be characterized by *fidelity, trust, *love and commitment. Marriage has traditionally functioned as the primary context for the *procreation and nurture of children, as well as providing for their well-being. In the Christian tradition, marriage is seen as a theological symbol, denoting in a metaphorical way the relationship between God and God's people, including Yahweh and Israel in the Old Testament, and Christ and the church in the New Testament. *See also* cohabitation; common-law marriage; divorce; monogamy; remarriage.

Marxism. The philosophical and social theories expounded by the socialist philosopher Karl Marx (1818-1883) and propagated by his followers. Marxism asserts that human *society is marked by a class struggle in which a privileged ruling class of capitalists, who control the means of production, exploits a working class, and that this fundamentally unjust economic situation results in humans being estranged from one another, from nature and from their own fundamental essence. Marxism looks to a day when this situation will give way to a utopian era characterized by a free and radically egalitarian human society. This society, however, can only arise through the struggle of the working class against their oppressors. Marxism declares that the socioeconomic structures of any given society condition its basic values, *laws, *customs and beliefs, and therefore that ethical systems are a reflection of class interest. Marxist ethics, therefore, seeks to advance the well-being of the working class, with the goal of transforming the world. *See also* economic system; exploitation; socialism.

masturbation. The act of stimulating one's own sexual organs. Whereas some ethicists advocate the practice as a way of avoiding sexual promiscuity, many in the Christian tradition view masturbation as immoral because it is not directed toward *procreation within the bonds of *marriage. A third group sees it as an inferior but not necessarily morally culpable practice, insofar as it belongs to a stage in the process of developing a healthy sexual identity.

medical ethics. The study of the moral ideals, rules and codes of conduct that govern the behavior of medical professionals. Medical ethics explores the relationships between practitioner, patient and institution with the intent of fostering medical care that is characterized by moral *integrity. A basic code of medical ethics is contained in the physician's Hippocratic Oath, which is often summarized in the dictum "do no *harm." *See also* professional ethics.

medieval ethics. The ethical reflection that characterized the Christian theologians, philosophers and church leaders in the Middle Ages. The medieval era witnessed the publication of moral treatises that drew not only from the Bible and the early church fathers but also from the ancient Greek philosophers, as well as Jewish and Islamic ethical literature (*see also* Islamic ethics; Jewish ethics). *Plato and *Aristotle's works on ethical theory were used as a framework to elucidate biblical moral views. Peter Abelard (1079-1142) was one of the first to use the term *ethics* for the category of moral philosophy. Medieval ethics is primarily teleological in nature, in that ethicists inquired regarding the nature of the ultimate end, *good or *telos* of human existence (*see also* teleological ethics). *Ethics, in turn, became the exploration of how humans should live in the light of that end.

meliorism. A stance, located between social or moral optimism and pessimism, that asserts that humans can and should make the world a better place. Sometimes credited to William James, meliorism maintains that humans are morally neither predominantly *evil nor *good, but that they are able to make life better regardless of the situation. Meliorism maintains that history is a record of the freeing of humankind from the bonds of superstitious belief and the ascendancy of the scientific method as the means for understanding nature and its past.

merit. As a general term, the quality of deserving praise, esteem or reward; as an ethical term, the entitlement to praise or reward on the basis of *right actions or the cultivation of *virtues; as a term in *Christian ethics, the idea that a person can acquire worth or standing before God through fulfilling certain requirements, through the use of innate abilities or through moral actions or conduct. The Reformers, such as Luther, rejected any suggestion that humans might merit *righteousness before God. As a consequence, *Reformation ethics has tended to describe the moral life as consisting in the reception of divine grace rather than the attempt to gain merit.

metaethics. A synonym for *analytical ethics, the aspect of philosophical or *general ethics that examines the nature and grounds of ethical beliefs. Metaethics includes the study of the meaning of ethical concepts such as "*right," "*good," "free," "responsible." It explores the various proposed methods of justifying moral assertions. It also raises the question of how *ethics itself can be rationally justified. Thus it asks, "Why be moral?"

metaphysical moralism. The theory of moral justification that declares that ethical statements can be translated into assertions of metaphysical or theological fact. Thus, **right* does not primarily mean "what is conducive to *happiness," but "what is commanded by God." In this sense, metaphysical moralism may be viewed as a variety of *naturalism, albeit one that appeals to the supernatural, rather than the natural realm. *See also* justification, moral; theological voluntarism.

middle axioms. In logic an axiom is defined as an assertion, the truth of which is not subject to proof but instead provides a basis for arguing for other assertions. In *ethics, a middle axiom is an ethical assertion that is obviously true but also appears to arise out of one or more fundamental axioms. For example, the truth of the injunction against *murder is not subject to proof, but serves as the basis for other principles of *personal ethics or *social ethics. Nevertheless, the injunction arises out of the more fundamental command to *love one's neighbor.

monogamy. The condition of having only one marital partner at any one time. Monogamy is practically universal in most Western countries. It is also a cornerstone of the Christian ideal of *marriage. The biblical case for monogamy arises out of the Old Testament narrative of Adam and Eve, which Jesus appropriated in his discussion of *divorce as indicating God's intention for marriage "from the beginning" (Mt 19:4-6). *See also* bigamy; polygamy.

moral argument. In Christian apologetics, the line of reasoning that deduces the existence of God from the moral nature of humankind. One famous formulation, that of Immanuel *Kant, argues that God is a necessary postulate of moral or "practical" reason. Kant's argument begins with the universal human sense of *duty or of being morally conditioned, from which he concludes that God must exist, if this experience of moral *obligation is to have any meaning. Moreover, in Kant's estimation, virtuous conduct in a truly moral universe must be rewarded and wrongdoing must be punished, a *principle that requires a supreme power who guarantees the ultimate moral outcome.

moral autonomy. The belief that moral direction is internal, arising through the operation of a principle resident within the individual moral agent. In the Enlightenment, the locus of moral *autonomy was believed to lie in the light of reason present within each human being, which in turn gave the individual access to universal *law written into the very structure of the universe.

moral development. The concept of moral development arises from the observation that human beings are not born morally mature. Four alternative theories of moral development have come to the fore in recent years. The psychoanalytic approach, proposed by Sigmund Freud, asserts that moral development coincides with the development of the personality in childhood (*see also* id, ego, superego). The social-learning approach posits that moral *standards are behavioral patterns learned directly through various socializing forces. The cognitive-structural approach, most fully explicated by Lawrence Kohlberg, asserts that moral *norms are imbedded in universal structures of social interaction, of which the concept of *justice is most basic. The character-formation approach posits that a person's moral life not only involves social structures and judgments, but also agency, understood as *intention, perception, hopes, *habits, values and *virtues (*see also* character). This fourth approach emphasizes the individual's *responsibility in moral development. *See also* education, moral; psychological ethics.

moralism. An outlook that views life in moral terms or understands life as moral in character. The term is often used to express the negative connotation of the rigid or excessive application of moral *principles, *laws or considerations to life situations.

morality, morals, moralize. From the Latin *mos* (adj. *moralis*) meaning *custom or usage, a synonym for *ethics. Morality involves determining what is to be believed to be *right and *good and then living out such beliefs. Morals, in turn, are the various *principles regarding right and wrong, viewed individually or as comprising a whole, that constitute a standard for conduct and are seen as governing the way humans are to live. Despite the affinity between the terms *morals* and *ethics* in philosophical treatments of the topic, in the media or in casual conversation, people today often distinguish between the two, so that morality comes to be linked to sentiments, personal preferences or scruples. As a consequence, *moralize* is often used in a pejorative sense to refer to the attempt to inculcate one's own moral conclusions on others.

mortal sin. In Roman Catholic theology, an act that so interferes with or opposes the working of divine *love that the one committing it is deemed deserving of eternal damnation. To be reckoned guilty of having committed a mortal *sin, the person must have performed an act that is gravely sinful with sufficient reflection and consent. A venial sin, in contrast, although condemnable, does not interfere or oppose the love of God to such a degree as to incur eternal damnation. *See also* guilt.

mortification. The process of engaging in an ascetic action of self-denial, based on the Pauline injunction to "put to death" selfish desires (Col 3:5), with the goal of identifying thereby more completely with Christ and his crucifixion (Gal 2:19-20). *See also* Paul, Pauline ethics.

murder. The unlawful killing of another person or being. Degrees of murder are distinguished in proportion to the deliberate and willful nature of the crime. *See also* homicide.

N

natural law. A *law presumed to be grounded in *nature itself. A natural law is a *norm for ethical behavior that is deemed binding on all humans because it coheres with the human essence (*see also* human nature) or with the structure of the universe, perhaps because it was legislated by God. The idea initially arose among the ancient Greeks and Romans, especially the *Stoics. But it came to the fore in the Christian tradition as thinkers drew from both philosophy and the Bible to devise a theory of *morality and *politics that could be understood to be universally applicable. Insofar as natural laws can be known by reason alone, without revelation, they provide guidance for all humans, and when followed they enhance the *common good, but also render each person morally responsible to a divine judge. In jurisprudence, natural law theory is invoked to set limits to the legislative prerogatives of rulers. In this sense, it forms an alternative to legal positivism, which suggests that human sovereigns are not subject to constraints from any higher court of appeal. *See also* natural rights.

natural rights. Entitlements with which humans are endowed by *nature or by virtue of their status as being human. These *rights are considered inalienable, universal and knowable through reason by all competent human beings. Moreover, the theory of natural rights asserts that rights accrue to humans directly, and thus independently of any rights-granting agency, such as the king, state, church or one's social class. The concept of natural rights was especially prominent in the Enlightenment era. *See also* civil rights; human rights; natural law.

naturalism, ethical. A theory of moral justification that asserts that ethical concepts such as "*good" and "*right" arise out of observable fact, what is or the way things are. The connection of ethical precepts to observable reality leads to the conclusion that ethical judgments can be empirically verified, at least in theory. Naturalism, therefore, links judgments about the right and the good to what is purported to be natural, and it proceeds from the assumption that humans can discover universal *principles of *obligation, because these are evident in the workings of the universe or in *human nature itself. *See also* justification, moral; naturalistic fallacy.

naturalistic fallacy. The erroneous assumption believed to be the Achilles heel of naturalism in its various permutations. In its simplest form, the argument declares that naturalism mistakenly assumes a connection between what is and what ought to be. But just as an "is" cannot be derived grammatically from an "ought," so also in *ethics one cannot assume that what is—even what is given in the universe—is what ought to be. G. E. Moore is often cited as casting this argument in its classic philosophical form. *See also* naturalism, ethical.

nature. The term *nature* can have several meanings: the entire physical universe in which human beings are embedded and function; the essence or essential character of a thing; an inborn tendency or disposition of a person or persons. These various understandings coalesce in the idea in *ethics that nature is a universal and unchangeable reality in accordance with which a person's conduct or moral standing can be measured. *See also* human nature; natural law; naturalistic fallacy.

Neo-Platonism. The last stage of the development of Greek philosophy in the ancient world, generally identified with *Plotinus. Neo-Platonists taught that everything emanates (flows) from the transcendent principle of "the One" and is destined to return to the One through a process of purification. According to Neo-Platonists, the *good life entails a flight from the material world and sense experience to an increasingly closer relationship to the ultimate principle, or the One. Matter for the Neo-Platonists was not neutral, but insofar as it was lacking of the *good, it was regarded as *evil (and hence evil in the sense of deprivation). Neo-Platonism greatly influenced certain early church thinkers, particularly Origen and *Augustine, and as a result seeped into the Western Christian intellectual tradition and formed a philosophical foundation for the kind of Christian mysticism that involved a strict asceticism and deprecated the material realm.

New Testament ethics. The study of the ethical teachings of the New Testament. The foundation for the ethic of the New Testament is the belief that Jesus of Nazareth is the Christ, the Son of God, and that he fulfilled the divine *righteousness. As a consequence, the heart of the New Testament ethic is Jesus, both as teacher and as master or Lord. The New Testament writers, in turn, sought to apply Jesus' teachings to the situations faced by the early Christian communities. But they also set forth an ethic of the *imitation of Christ and of devotion to Christ that looked to the indwelling Spirit of Christ as the agent of transformation in the individual, in the *community and, by extension, throughout the world. *See also* Jesus, ethic of; Paul, Pauline ethics.

nihilism. A term attributed to the fifth-century B.C. Athenian philosopher Gorgias, who posited that "nothing exists, and if it did, it could not be known." Nihilism, as a moral philosophy, postulates that ethical *norms cannot be justified rationally and that the inevitable result is despair in the face of the emptiness of life. The late modern era witnessed the rise of several varieties of nihilism. Friedrich Nietzsche, for example, differentiated between a passive nihilism that stops at despair and an active form that attempts to clear away false moralities in anticipation of the appearance of something superior.

noncognitivism, nondescriptivism. A theory of moral justification that denies that ethical judgments carry cognitive meaning. Foundational to the noncognitivist position is the assumption that a statement is meaningful only if it asserts or denies something that is objectively true or false about an object in the universe, so that its truth or falsity can be determined by comparing it with reality. The positive form of noncognitivism is sometimes termed *emotivism. *See also* justification, moral.

nonconflicting absolutism. A theory of *deontological ethics that asserts that the rightness of actions is determined by a set of absolute moral *principles that in actuality never collide. Hence, the moral agent is never placed in a situation in which one such absolute must be transgressed in order to obey another. *See also* absolute, absolutism.

nondescriptivism. *See* noncognitivism.

nonnaturalism. *See* intuitionism.

nonresistance. Similar to, but not synonymous with *pacifism, the teaching that humans ought to abstain from any form of violence even to the point of eschewing forcefully resisting aggressors or perpetrators of injustice. As a positive ethic, the theory asserts that social change is best advanced through passive nonresistance, rather than active resistance, and that *nonviolence is an effective means of protest. Christian proponents claim that in the *Sermon on the Mount, Jesus called his disciples to nonresistance as a central aspect of a transforming ethic of *love. Most Christians who take Jesus' call seriously tend to practice a passive resistance by abstaining from violence or active resistance, while still refusing to obey laws or orders that they believe conflict with the teachings of Jesus.

nonviolence. Similar to *nonresistance, a form of *civil disobedience that is vigorous and principled, yet does not encourage or participate in violence. In the twentieth century, several religious leaders, including Gandhi and Martin Luther King Jr., promoted a militant nonviolence as a means of social protest with the goal of effecting social change.

norm. As an ethical term, a rule, *law or *principle that governs, directs or prescribes some aspect of moral conduct; a standard against which moral conduct or *character is measured. Ethicists sometimes distinguish between absolute norms and contingent norms, the former being those that are applicable in all situations, whereas the latter apply only when some other factor is present. An additional distinction can be made between universal and role norms, in that the former are incumbent on all persons; in contrast, the latter apply only to certain groups of persons or when a person is functioning in a certain role, such as serving as a medical doctor. *See also* absolute, absolutism; normative ethics.

normative ethics. As the word **norm* suggests, normative ethics is the division of philosophical or *general ethics that has as its goal the formulation of *standards or *principles for human conduct, i.e., ethical norms. Normative ethics sets forth judgments about what is *right, *good or obligatory, and it offers reasons for such judgments. *See also* judgments, types of.

nuclear energy. The use of atomic fission as a power-generating source. Nuclear energy has been a topic of ethical debate, in part because of the far-reaching consequences associated with the potential problems involved in its production. These include reactor meltdown, spent-fuel disposal, worker safety and collateral radioactive contamination of the community.

nuclear warfare. The use of atomic fission or fusion weapons in a variety of tactical or strategic configurations. Nuclear warfare introduces ethical considerations beyond those connected with conventional warfare in that their use carries the potential for catastrophic results not only for the intended target but for entire populations, ecosystems and possibly even major parts of the earth. Terms such as "mutually assured destruction" and "nuclear winter" are frequently used to refer to the results of an exchange of nuclear weapons between combatants. Some ethicists conclude that the advent of the nuclear age has made the *just war theory obsolete. Others, however, point to the deterrent effect of nuclear weapons as a justification for their continued deployment.

O

oaths. *See* swearing.

obedience. The willing compliance to a specific *commandment, prohibition, *law or *duty, or to a set of teachings. Most philosophical and religious ethical traditions emphasize a properly directed obedience as a *virtue. The Christian conception of obedience arises out of a more fundamental theological *principle, namely, the recognition that inherent in God as the sovereign creator is the prerogative to command and therefore to demand obedience from humans. At the same time, the Bible portrays God as acting on behalf of humankind by entering into covenant with humans. Viewed from this perspective, obedience becomes the appropriate human response to the divine initiative, rather than slavish submission to a supreme lawgiver.

obligation. As an ethical term, a *responsibility or claim upon a person's life, demeanor or conduct that is morally binding. Although it is generally seen as a synonym for **duty, obligation* is occasionally used in a wider sense to include not only mandatory actions but also dispositions that are incumbent upon a moral agent.

Old Testament ethics. Ethical reflection in the Old Testament displays three factors that set the Hebrews apart from other Ancient Near Eastern peoples: the focus on Yahweh as the sole Creator, on

Yahweh's *holiness and on Yahweh's election of Israel. As a result, Old Testament ethics reflects both a priestly and a prophetic dimension. Whereas the priestly dimension emphasizes God as Creator, the prophetic dimension highlights Israel's fluctuating relationship to God due to the nation's inability to live up to the demand for holiness inherent in their status as God's covenant partner. Past failures led the prophets to anticipate a day when God would reign over all the earth, a vision of the future that they saw as having moral implications for life in the present. *See also* Jewish ethics.

oppression. The use of *force, coercion or authority to constrain the *freedom of another; the subjection of a person or group of people to injustice or *tyranny. Oppression generally involves the violation of the *rights of others, whether in the form of *exploitation or the denial of *justice, and it may be understood in contrast to both freedom and *social justice. Oppression may be religious, social, economic or political. Repeatedly the biblical writers call for an end to oppression and the establishment of social justice, and Jesus viewed his own ministry in this light (e.g., Lk 4:18-19).

organ transplant. A medical procedure by which the failed organ of a recipient is replaced with the healthy organ of a genetically matched donor or, in some circumstances, of a person who has recently died. Many ethicists regard organ transplanting as a means whereby health can be restored to someone who would otherwise suffer ill effects or even death. It also provides a way in which one person can show *love to someone who is in need. In the case of cadaveric donation, it is a way in which a gift of life can be offered to another even in the face of one's own *death. Some religious ethicists, in contrast, aver that the prolongation of life through organ transplantation is an infringement on God's sovereignty over all life. Moreover, live donation carries a degree of risk to the donor. Organ transplanting involving either live or deceased donors can foster a mercenary spirit or a climate of injustice if payment for donation is offered as an inducement. Cadaveric donation can set up a *conflict of interest between care of a potential donor who is dying and the desire to prolong the patient's life for the sake of potential organ recipients. Finally, the question also arises as to whether under certain circumstances an organ transplant is the best use of medical resources.

original sin. As a theological term, the universal participation of human beings in the fall of Adam. Two questions debated by theologians have important ethical implications: Does original sin mean that humans inherit a propensity to sin, or is *sin transmitted merely through the socialization process? Does original sin mean that humans are born guilty before God, or does a person first incur *guilt through the act of willful sin? Regardless of the answers to these questions, the doctrine of original sin has stamped *Christian ethics with a unique perspective on the nature of the moral quest. According to Christian teaching, humans cannot attain moral *righteousness, moral renewal or the *telos* of their existence through human efforts alone or through the employment of human resources alone. Instead, the goal of the moral quest requires divine intervention, the transforming power of the Spirit and the reception of divinely offered grace. *See also* human nature.

P

pacifism. An ethical stance, closely connected but not synonymous with *nonviolence and *nonresistance, that eschews the use of physical *force or violence—especially in the form of *war—to combat *evil, aggression or injustice, or to attain just goals. Pacifists vary in the extent to which they see the *principle of nonviolence as applicable to human social interaction. Some limit the principle to war, whereas others extend it to include armed police forces, private possession of weapons and even the use of personal physical force. In addition, some pacifists invoke nonviolence only in cases of aggression against their own person, but would condone the use of force to restrain an aggressor from injuring someone else. Most historians agree that pacifism was the prevailing position in the church prior to Constantine. Even though it subsequently gave way to *just war theories, it continued to be followed in monasticism and became a central tenet of the Anabaptists in the radical Reformation as well as the Quakers in England. Until recent years, pacifism has been consistently advocated by the Mennonites. *See also* conscientious objection; disarmament.

paternalism. The practice of government by paternal administration; the attempt to govern in a manner analogous to the way in which a father regulates the life of his *family within a patriarchal system. Paternalism arises out of an attitude that looks upon a nation, *community or group in a manner similar to a father's view of his family. More specifically, paternalism entails acting in a manner that limits the *autonomy or liberty of another and that proceeds without regard to the current desires or values of the other, but has as its purpose the promotion of the *good of or the prevention of *harm to the other. In addition to its outworking in the political realm, the paternalistic attitude has influenced the manner in which many persons have understood the moral injunctions to *love one's family, one's neighbor and, in the case of the helping professions, the patient. In his essay *On Liberty,* John Stuart Mill eschews paternalism as morally problematic. Mill notes that paternalism tends to violate the *principle of autonomy and can actually do harm to the dignity of the individual. Consequently, many ethical theorists today advocate at best a weak paternalism.

patriotism. A passionate allegiance to one's nation or *community, together with a devotion to its institutions, a fervent loyalty to its values, a profound sense of attachment to its symbols and people, and a concern for its future welfare. The Christian ethical tradition displays a mixed stance toward patriotism. Some Christians have been characterized by a keen sense of patriotism, sometimes on the basis of a belief that the nation or *society to which they belong has a special role in the work of God in history. Others have seen patriotism as undercutting the disciple's primary loyalty to Christ and undermining the universal or international character of the church. Some have even equated patriotism with idolatry.

patristic ethics. The ethical teachings of the Greek and Latin church leaders from the late first through the fourth centuries. The ethical writings of the church fathers vary considerably, due to geographical location, intellectual and theological formation, social setting and the various methods used to interpret Scripture. Prior to the rule of Constantine and the cessation of *persecution, the patristic leaders were especially interested in such issues as *pacifism, martyrdom, the avoidance of pagan conduct and the general pattern of moral instruction found in the Jewish heritage. The mandate to *love is probably the most recurrent theme in patristic ethics.

Paul, Pauline ethics. Paul sought to understand the significance of Jesus' entire life, ministry, death, resurrection and exaltation for ethical living. He also attempted to apply Jesus' teachings to the situations faced by the early churches under his care. Central to Paul's teaching was the belief that the Christian life was marked by union with Christ and hence by the indwelling presence of the Holy Spirit, which taken together constitute believers as a new creation. His training as a Pharisee made Paul well aware of the rigid demands of the *law as interpreted by the teachers of his day. Paul realized that the only way in which the requirements of the law could be met was through union with Jesus Christ, who had fulfilled the law, and by the transforming power of the Spirit within, who brings about a new reality characterized by growing conformity to the royal law of *love. Paul's ethic was also directed toward living in the era between the historic act of Christ on Calvary and the consummation of history at Christ's return. Paul's writings were contextual, designed to address concrete situations. Yet underlying them all is a Spirit-driven, love-focused, new creation-based, eschatologically oriented ethic. *See also* eschatology, its role in ethics; New Testament ethics.

peace. As an ethical term, the absence of conflict; the cessation of hostilities; or—based on the Hebrew concept of *shalom*—the positive condition of personal or communal wholeness, *integrity and well-being. In the Christian tradition, the pursuit of peace and the attempt to be an agent of peace are viewed as indispensable aspects of the Christian calling, in keeping with Jesus' *beatitude "blessed are the peacemakers" (Mt 5:9). An ethical issue that emerges from the quest for peace is that of the relationship between peace and *justice: Should peace be deemed a greater *good or a higher goal than justice?

pederasty, pedophilia. Pederasty and pedophilia denote sexual intimacy between an adult and a child, although the first term refers more specifically to liaisons involving male adults and children, whereas the second is a more general term denoting any adult-child sexual activity. Many of the ancient Greek philosophers sanctioned a form of the practice. Nevertheless, today all such activities are generally deemed inappropriate, in part because of the *harm such behavior can inflict on the participants, especially the child, for whom sexual activity at a young age can arrest or disrupt normal physical and emotional development. Moreover, because of the immaturity of the child and the unequal *power differential between the adult and the child, the child is not in a position to give *informed consent to the liaison. In the case of the adult, engaging in sexual activity with a child is both a possible sign of and can lead to psychological and sexual maladjustment. Finally, many Christians view pederasty as a violation of God's intention for the expression of human sexuality. *See also* sexuality, sexual ethics.

penology. The study or philosophy of *punishment; the exploration of the punishment of *crime, the rehabilitation of criminals and prison management. Penologists sometimes divide punishment into two main types according to its purpose, whether retributive or utilitarian. The ethical issues associated with penology include the justification of punishment in its various forms, including the question of the *morality of *capital punishment, and the nature of just treatment of prisoners, together with the desirability of *prison reform. More recently, the question of the universal applicability of theories of punishment has arisen, especially in the context of the impulse toward implementing culturally sensitive or perhaps even traditional cultural ways of dealing with crimes in cases in which the perpetrator is a member of a visible minority. *See also* juvenile ethics; restitution, retribution.

perfectionism. As a theological term, a teaching, sometimes known as entire *sanctification and often associated with John Wesley and the Wesleyan theological tradition, that declares that moral perfection can be attained in this life. The basis of the idea lies in the biblical injunctions to be perfect as God is perfect (Mt 5:48), holy as God is holy (Lev 19:2; 1 Pet 1:15-16) or move toward perfection (Heb 6:1). Although some proponents suggest that a Christian can attain complete sinlessness (1 Jn 3:6), perfectionism is more generally understood to mean either that by God's grace a Christian can overcome the dominion of *sin or that by the working of the Spirit a Christian can be made perfect in love for God (although some add that a person can fall from this state).

persecution. The act of inflicting unjust harassment or injury on a person or group of people, ostensibly because the victim espouses beliefs or engages in practices that are contrary to those held by the dominant social group or out of favor with the governing authorities. Generally the perpetrators believe that they are morally justified in engaging in such acts, insofar as they view themselves as acting in the best interests of truth, the *common good or even the victims themselves.

personal ethics. The study of the moral *principles that ought to inform the conduct of the individual human as well as the application of such principles to aspects of the life of the individual. Personal ethics is generally seen as considering the *habits, practices, and conduct of an individual moral agent, rather than of groups of people. Personal ethics is sometimes limited to practices of individuals that are not directed explicitly toward others, and are considered apart from the person's relationships to others. Hence, personal ethics might address questions such as the propriety of smoking or consuming alcohol, and do so in a manner that focuses on their rightness or wrongness as they pertain to the life of the individual himself or herself. Although the effects of such practices on others might also be a consideration, in personal ethics the chief interest is the *holiness of the individual moral agent. Personal ethics is often contrasted with *social ethics.

personalism. A philosophical perspective that asserts that all reality is ultimately personal, that experience of oneself as a personal being is the starting point of knowledge, and that personhood is the source and locus of value. One variety of personalism, personal realism, declares that ultimate reality is spiritual and supernatural, although it recognizes the existence of a natural, nonmental order as well. Personalism also emphasizes the unity of the subjective and objective aspects of reality. As a defined philosophical school, personalism was especially strong in the United States, principally at Boston University, in the late nineteenth and early twentieth centuries. Its impact, however, extends to the present and is evident in the work of such thinkers as John Macmurray, who views the person as essentially social.

philosophical ethics. *See* general ethics.

pietism. A Bible-oriented, experiential approach to Christian life that emphasizes personal appropriation of *faith and sees the concern for a life characterized by *holiness as more important than mere adherence to formal theology (doctrine) and church order.

Initially, pietism was a movement within the Lutheran Church in Germany that sought to correct the reduction of the faith to mere assent to doctrine, which the pietists believed led to "dead orthodoxy." Philip Jacob Spener (1635-1705) is often cited as the father of German Pietism. Spener sought to bring about change in the church by founding small groups of pious believers *(collegia pietatis)* who met for mutual edification. Eventually, the emphasis on holy living that characterized pietism fostered a heightened preoccupation with ridding oneself of *sin by refusing to engage in popular pastimes that were deemed worldly.

Plato, Platonic ethics. The ethical teaching associated with the ancient Greek philosopher Plato (428-348 B.C.). Plato's ethic could be characterized as one of ordered integration or harmony. He asserted that the goal of life is to actualize one's true nature together with one's many innate potentialities. For Plato, the highest good is the well-ordered whole to which each part contributes according to its own capacity. This quest for the ordered life led Plato to his understanding of *virtue. Plato outlined four primary, integrated virtues, each of which corresponded to a specific function of the soul: *wisdom, corresponding to reason; *courage, corresponding to *will; *temperance, corresponding to desire; and *justice as the integrative virtue. For Plato, the integrative virtue of justice linked the individual with *society. Plato's understanding of the *good comes from his metaphysical concept of forms. Every reality is an exemplar of a corresponding eternal form. Standing at the apex of the forms is the "form of the good." A thing in reality is good insofar as it participates in and corresponds to the form of the good. *See also* cardinal virtues.

pleasure. As a general term, an agreeable sensation or the sense of enjoyment. Throughout the history of *ethics, pleasure has been and remains a central topic of reflection. *Aristotle differentiated between a momentary pleasure that is experienced in varying degrees of intensity only for a finite length of time and pleasure as a set disposition or manner of viewing the world, such as evidenced when a person takes pleasure in a moral *virtue or in *friendship. Some ethicists elevate pleasure as the highest *good, a theory known as *hedonism. Like their counterparts in the philosophical tradition, Christian ethicists have been divided over the status of pleasure. Some propose a kind of Christian hedonism, whereas others contrast the quest for pleasure with the biblical teaching that a person's chief desire ought to be God's reign and *righteousness. *See also* eudaemonism; happiness.

Plotinus (A.D. 205-270). The chief proponent and expositor of *Neo-Platonism. Plotinus's philosophy exemplifies the alteration of *Plato indicative of Neo-Platonism as a whole, namely, the idea that matter is not merely lacking in *goodness, but is *evil, and that the influence of the body is the cause of all the evil in the soul's existence. Moreover, he taught that because all thought involves duality, the unity lying behind all reality can be apprehended only as thought is transcended by means of an ecstatic union with the unifying principle, known as "the One." Plotinus understood the virtuous life in relation to the soul's ascent to the One. In his estimation, the civil *virtues—*prudence, *courage, *temperance and rectitude (*justice)—which facilitate living in the world of multiplicity, must be cultivated from the perspective of their role in facilitating union with the One.

pluralism. As a general term, the outlook characterized by the advocacy and embrace of the presence of variety and diversity. As a philosophical term, pluralism is the perspective that elevates the categories of diversity, multiplicity and difference, rather than homogeneity, unity and sameness. In social theory, pluralism is the celebration of a social system that promotes the presence, *autonomy and ongoing development of diverse religious, ethnic, racial and social groups within the system. Pluralism as a stance in theology is the belief that there are many paths to and expressions of truth about God, and several equally valid means to salvation. In *ethics, pluralism generally refers to the belief that all moral principles arise out of a particular *community that espouses them, and that in any *society that includes a multiplicity of moral communities a plurality of possibly competing ethical systems will exist simultaneously. Pluralists often add that because an act or *principle of action can only be judged from within the context of the particular community that espouses it, there is no universal standpoint from which to adjudicate the debate among moral communities or to determine definitively which ethical system is valid. Some pluralists conclude from this situation that the various ethical systems are equally valid. *See also* conventionalism; relativism; tolerance; universal moral judgments.

politics. The organized conduct of and various attempts to regulate relationships that exist within any form of human *community. Politics, however, is generally used in the narrower sense of denoting the science and art of governing human *society or the citizens of any human community or nation. The word *politics* originates from the Latin *politicus* and the Greek *politikos*, both of which mean "a resident of a city" or "a citizen." Politics not only embraces governance but is also used to refer to the tactics, methods and schemes (sometimes unethical) used in governing. *See also* power; public policy.

polygamy. The state or condition of having multiple spouses at one time. Although polygamy remains a widespread practice today, nations that have been influenced by Christianity tend to see *monogamy as the ideal. Polygamy was also practiced in the Old Testament, but it was never enjoined by the biblical writers as the ideal. Some commentators believe that the stipulation "the husband of one wife" found among the Pauline qualifications for offices in the church (1 Tim 3:2, 12 NRSV note) was directed against the practice of polygamy as it was found in the ancient Roman Empire. *See also* bigamy; marriage.

population ethics. The division of *ethics that explores the moral questions surrounding the numerical size, growth, environmental impact and distribution of humans on the earth as a whole or in any particular region. Population ethics gained importance in recent decades due to the concern that the earth's resources may not be able to sustain unlimited growth in the human population. As a consequence of this concern, discussions within the field of population ethics tend to focus on issues regarding population control, such as government regulated *family size, government sponsored *birth control, volunteer family planning and responsible parenthood. Population ethics also tackles the ethical dimensions of problems associated with large populations, including malnutrition, *famine, *poverty and consequent environmental quality (*ecology).

pornography. Writings, photographs or purported works of art that purposely depict illicit sexual acts or intimate sexual activity in a perverse manner. The term is also often used to refer to pictures that present a person in a sexually seductive nude or partially nude pose. A pornographic work debases human sexual expression and exploits human sexual passions. The word is a transliteration of a Greek term derived from *pornē* (prostitute) and *graphē* (writing). According to the U.S. Supreme Court, to be deemed pornographic a work must be "devoid of redeeming social value." Many pornographic works combine the erotic with other themes, such as aggression, with the goal of triggering sexual arousal in the audience. A work of pornography may also have as its intention to challenge the normative status of the view that the sexual relationship is to be characterized by loving intimacy. Pornography is generally characterized as either "soft core" or "hard core," the latter designating works that depict the most vulgar and base of sexual acts. Although some ethicists argue that pornography is guaranteed by the right to freedom of speech, others favor placing limits on its creation and propagation on the basis of such considerations as its potential detrimental effects on *society as a whole as well as its dehumanizing quality. *See also* censorship.

postmodern ethics. The approach to the ethical task that takes seriously and builds from the concerns integral to the postmodern context or that incorporates aspects of postmodernism. Postmodernism denotes a variety of intellectual and cultural developments in Western *society that have their philosophical roots in nineteenth-century Romanticism but blossomed in the late twentieth century. The postmodern ethos is characterized by a rejection of modernist values and a mistrust of the supposedly universal rational *principles developed in the Enlightenment era. Postmoderns generally place high value in the diversity of philosophical outlooks and religious traditions that characterizes contemporary society. The postmodern turn has led to a widespread embracing of ethical *pluralism. In addition, it has fostered a renewed interest in the *ethic of being, with its attendant aspects such as the cultivation of *virtues and the quest for spirituality, an awareness of the communal nature of *ethics, and an appeal to narrative thought as providing a way of understanding the connection between ethics, or *moral development, and personal identity formation.

poverty. The condition of being in want of the basic necessities of life. Poverty is sometimes defined by means of income, hence, as the situation of not having sufficient income to sustain life. Alternatively, poverty can be defined by appeal to one's economic status in comparison to others in *society. Thus, (relative) poverty is the condition of deprivation that arises when one's economic quality of life (*see* life, quality of) is below accepted *standards of well-being. As an ethical concept, poverty can refer to a voluntary condition in which the person forgoes the possession of material goods and *property as one aspect of a vocational life. Poverty can also denote an involuntary situation that may be due to personal or social realities such as unemployment, mental or physical infirmity, or *oppression. The Christian tradition has generally seen poverty, in the sense of being destitute of the basic necessities of life, as an ethical concern. This stance is based both on particular biblical injunctions to minister to persons in need as well as on the biblical vision of the *kingdom of God: When God comes to reign, all persons share in the bounty of the earth.

power. The capacity or ability to effect specific outcomes. Viewed from the ethical perspective, power, understood as the mere ability to accomplish something or reach an intended result, must be differentiated from authority, which may be defined as the right to use power. The question of what constitutes the just exercise of power has long been a topic of *ethics. In this context, the Christian tradition generally views God as the one in whom rests ultimate authority to exercise power. As a consequence, human power is ultimately derived from God, for which reason humans are ultimately accountable to God for the manner in which they use the power entrusted to them. *See also* force; politics.

pragmatism. As a philosophical concept, an epistemological theory that assumes that every truth or idea has practical consequences and that these practical consequences are a critical test of its truthfulness. Some pragmatists add that there are no transcendental sources of truth; therefore, truth and values are relative to their usefulness to either individuals or societies. Pragmatists such as William James regard the world as ethically neutral but capable of being improved. In *ethics, pragmatism is sometimes associated with *utilitarianism, insofar as both appeal to results in the process of making moral judgments.

praxis. A term taken directly from the Greek, literally meaning "deed, action or activity." The basis for its contemporary use lies in two ideas: first, theoretical reflection arises out of active commitment, and therefore the criterion for right thinking (orthodoxy) is right action (orthopraxis); second, in turn, the goal of right thinking is the transformation of the world. Praxis denotes the kind of active commitment that leads to theoretical reflection. The use of praxis in this sense seeks to bring about the uniting of, or the overcoming of, such conceptual dualities as theory and practice, belief and action, or commitment and its ethical outworking. Praxis is especially important as an ethical concept in *liberation ethics.

prejudice. As a general term, a preconceived opinion; the result of the act of judging without due examination of the relevant considerations. Although a prejudice, understood in this general sense, can be a favorable disposition, it is most often used to denote a negative or unfavorable judgment about an idea, thing or person. Moreover, the term can also be used to denote an unreasonable judgment in the sense of an opinion that is accepted despite clear or even overwhelming evidence to the contrary. This leads to the ethical sense in which the term is used, in which it is nearly synonymous with bigotry or *racism. Thus, prejudice refers to the (generally) negative attitude toward a person or group of people that is formed on the basis of preconceptions, unsubstantiated claims made by others, gossip or hearsay, and without due regard to what may actually be true regarding the person or group. Prejudice readily leads to *discrimination and hostile, injurious or unjust actions, or *persecution against the person or members of the group. In the Christian tradition, prejudice is often viewed as a violation of the injunction against bearing false witness, as well as running counter to the biblical ideal of treating others justly. Above all, however, it is seen as contrary to the ethic of *love. Finally, Christian ethicists often claim that the Christian vocation as peacemakers demands that Christians work to combat prejudice and its effects.

prescriptivism. Sometimes defined as the theory that *morality entails the conformity of actions to preestablished *laws or ideals. It is, however, more often used to refer to a variety of *noncognitivism, namely, the theory of moral justification that views ethical statements as expressions of feeling (*see also* emotivism). Prescriptivists add that the goal of such expressions (i.e., ethical language) is not merely to voice personal feeling but also to guide the choices of others. Thus, ethical judgments are personal evaluations, recommendations or prescriptions that embody an implicit evaluation as well as an *imperative directed toward the hearer.

prima facie duty. *Prima facie* is a Latin term that means, literally, "first appearance" or "at first view," and hence, "based on the first impression." Prima facie evidence is evidence that is taken to establish a fact unless it is refuted, and thus such evidence carries the presumption of fact. As an ethical term, a prima facie *duty is a moral *obligation that is sensed intuitively by the moral agent as having a moral basis or as being ethically binding. In the ethical systems of *rule-deontologism, the idea expresses one proposed basis for adjudicating among a variety of possibly competing moral *principles. In such situations, the moral agent must look first to fulfilling prima facie duties, or more specifically the highest or most compelling prima facie duty (the "actual duty"), for these arise prior to, and thus have primacy over, other duties. *See also* hierarchicalism; intuition.

principle. As an ethical term, a general precept, rule of thumb or value that is deemed authoritative in moral discourse or is invoked to guide moral activity. Moral principles are sometimes contrasted to rules, in that the latter are seen to be concrete and applicable to specific actions, whereas the latter, being abstract and general, provide only guidelines for action. This distinction, however, is of limited usefulness. Ethicists also sometimes distinguish two basic types of moral principles: Categorical principles (such as "always act lovingly") delineate the duties incumbent on human moral agents; whereas definitional principles (such as "*love does not terminate the life of a fetus") connect these general duties to the types of situations that human agents might encounter.

principle monism. A *rule-deontologism approach to moral reasoning that declares that the whole of *morality can be founded on one supreme ethical *principle. Principle monism asserts that the rightness or wrongness of any act can be determined on the basis of whether or not it is in keeping with some central rule or principle of conduct. Proponents are divided, however, over the identity of this governing rule or principle. *See also* categorical imperative; Kant, Immanuel.

prison reform. The desire, based on ethical considerations, to bring about positive change in the manner in which *society treats persons convicted of criminal offenses. In the strict sense, prison reform focuses on the correctional methods used by and the conditions found in correctional institutions. Its chief concerns then are for the humane treatment of prisoners and the presence of programs designed to reform prison inmates and prepare them to become contributing members of society. In its wider sense, however, prison reform seeks to increase the effectiveness of the justice system by looking to alternatives to the current focus on retribution. Thus, some reformists advocate the increased use of methods that promote reconciliation between the convicted perpetrator and the victim or the family of the victim. Others propose the introduction into the justice system of methods gleaned from aboriginal peoples, especially in dealing with crimes committed by persons from tribal backgrounds. *See also* penology; restitution, retribution.

privacy. The condition in which access to a person or information about a person and a person's possessions by another person or institution are limited or severely curtailed. That privacy is a right is a hallmark of most Western ethical and political thought. The right to privacy is rooted in a particular understanding of the nature of personhood that views a person as being both boundaried and worthy of having such boundaries protected from encroachment. In this sense, the right to privacy is seen as insuring the integrity of personhood. The right to privacy, in turn, informs discussions regarding other dimensions of human personal and social relationships, including *confidentiality and *informed consent. A standing ethical debate in political thought concerns the extent to which the right to privacy ought to be upheld. According to some theorists, the right to privacy must be guarded with due diligence, in that it is constantly being threatened by the encroachments of a variety of institutions, including governmental, corporate and religious. Others aver that the right to privacy is not an *absolute, but that it must always be held in tension with a concern for the *common good, and therefore a person's privacy can be temporarily suspended in circumstances in which it is used as a cloak for such threats to *society as criminal behavior.

probabilism. A *principle, especially prominent among Jesuit proponents of *casuistry and articulated in the Latin phrase *lex dubia non obligat,* that states that a person is released from an *obligation when thorough investigation fails to dispel uncertainty regarding the moral status of the proposed obligation. Some ethicists restate the principle in a positive form as declaring that an action may be performed without incurring moral culpability if the agent has probable reason to believe that it is legitimate or has a seemingly valid moral rationale in favor of it. Another reformulation of the principle declares that in a case of sincere doubt, the course of action that favors liberty may be followed. Critics aver that probabilism promotes moral laxity, for it means that an individual's decision to act or to dismiss an obligation can be based on a single expression of probable doubt by an authoritative moralist. Moreover, the circumstances endemic to nearly every situation are so complex as to produce some measure of doubt about any prescribed *duty or course of action.

procreation. The act of creating offspring through sexual intercourse. In the Bible, procreation is viewed as a manner in which humans act on behalf of the Creator (e.g., Gen 1:28). Although in the narrow sense procreation refers to the act of begetting children, it is sometimes used in a broader manner to encompass the entire process of parental care for children within the context of *marriage, *family and home. In the Roman Catholic tradition, procreation is viewed as the chief goal of marriage, a position challenged by many Protestants. The advent of medically assisted insemination has introduced questions regarding the importance of sexual intercourse and marriage to the act of procreation. *See also* birth control; reproductive technologies; sexuality, sexual ethics.

professional ethics. The subdiscipline of *ethics that explores the ethical dimensions connected with engaging in a vocation or occupation. Although broadly understood, professional ethics encompasses the various fields of endeavor in which humans *work, it is generally seen as applying more narrowly to those vocations that are governed by a prescribed or assumed standard of conduct that forms the basis of determining not only the competence but also the moral rectitude of the person engaged in the occupation (e.g., doctors, nurses, lawyers, teachers). These vocations come under special scrutiny in part because the performance of the duties incumbent on practitioners involves a high level of trust between the professional person and the client, as well as a potential *power differential between them. Professional ethics raises such overarching questions as the ethical ramifications of the profession itself, the ethical implications of the phenomenon of professionalization and what comprises ethical living within the context of the profession. But its more specific mandate is to explore the practical matters associated with the practice of a profession, including the ethical ramifications of the professional-client relationship, as well as the application to the profession of issues such as *informed consent and *confidentiality.

propaganda. The reproduction and dissemination of information, an idea, an opinion or a proposed course of action with the goal of assisting or damaging a cause, person, group, organization or other institution. Propaganda has gained a negative connotation in that it is used to refer to the use of persuasive methods that circumvent critical reflection on the part of the hearers and thereby have as their intention the manipulation or control of a group, *society or nation.

property. Any item that an individual or business may acquire, possess, use and dispose. Although the term *property* is sometimes used in the narrow sense of real estate, it actually encompasses fixed assets, such as land; movable assets, such as material possessions; and intellectual property, which generally can be protected through the process of *copyright. The right to own property, or property rights, refers to the legal right to own property. The biblical perspective on property begins with God's ultimate ownership of all things as Creator and God's commitment of the earth to human *stewardship. The Christian tradition has displayed a variety of views regarding property *rights. Perhaps the most widely held position has acknowledged the right to private property as being a fundamental *human right, although some Christian groups have advocated communal ownership of all land and most goods (e.g., Acts 4:32-35). In either case, Christian ethicists have generally agreed that property rights are not absolute, but can be set aside when the *common good is at stake, and that personal property is to be used for the benefit of others as well as oneself. *See also* collectivism.

prostitution. The practice of engaging in sexual acts for compensation or financial gain. Although prostitution remains illegal in most localities, some ethicists are calling for its regulation by government legal structures so that some of its evil effects, including crimes of violence perpetrated against prostitutes and the spread of venereal disease, can be mitigated. In the Christian tradition, prostitution is condemned as a misappropriation of God's intention for human sexuality (cf. 1 Cor 6:15-17), as well as demeaning of both parties to the act, each of whom views the other as a commodity rather than as a person. *See also* sexuality, sexual ethics.

prudence. A *virtue that entails practical *wisdom or the ability to adapt appropriate means wisely in order to reach a *good or beneficial goal, especially through the exercise of foresight. Prudence was often listed among the *cardinal virtues in classical Greek philosophy, but it has been praised by Christian thinkers as well. *Augustine, for example, defined prudence as *love distinguishing with sagacity between what hinders it and what helps it. *Thomas Aquinas understood prudence as the intellectual virtue that directs a person to the choice of the right means to a proper end. In recent years, prudence has been used in the narrower sense of cautious wisdom or the exercise of discretion or careful reflection prior to acting. It has also been erroneously associated with prudishness.

psychological ethics. The study of how moral capacities develop in the person and how scientific knowledge about the human psyche informs judgments about the *right and the *good. Hence, psychological ethics explores the psychological aspects of the human moral capacity as well as the process by which moral behavior develops. *See also* moral development.

public policy. The decisions of a government regarding or affecting the relationships or interactions among the persons and institutions under its jurisdiction; the social goals that a particular government officially advocates or seeks to foster. Public policy encompasses both procedural and regulatory decisions, as well as decisions of substance. Political ethicists debate the extent to which the promotion of *morality is a legitimate function of government and hence ought to be an aspect of public policy. The movement in recent decades in most Western nations has been to reduce the involvement of government in areas deemed either to belong to the realm of private morality or to represent the moral perspective of one religious tradition (e.g., *blue laws, Sunday laws), while retaining an interest in matters deemed to pertain to the public welfare. *See also* politics.

punishment. The act of intentionally inflicting deprivation or pain on a person by someone who has either the *power or also the authority to do so; any form of legal penalty that is painful or unpleasant to the recipient, imposed as a response to an offense committed against the *norms of a *society. Ethicists are divided regarding the manner in which punishment may be justified. Perhaps the most common understanding is the retributive approach, in which punishment is justified as an intrinsic *good; that is, it is administered because it is what the offender deserves (*see also* intrinsic value). The major alternative is the consequentialist approach, in which punishment is justified as an extrinsic good. It is administered with a view toward some goal or result, such as the restoration of the offender to society or the deterrence of future crimes, whether by the offender or by members of society as a whole. *See also* capital punishment; corporal punishment; penology; restitution, retribution.

Puritans. A group of religious devotees who sought to purify the Church of England after the English Reformation (*see also* Reformation ethics). Foundational to Puritan ethics were the Calvinist doctrines regarding divine sovereignty, human depravity (*see also* total depravity) and the covenantal relationship between God and humans. To these the Puritans added an interest in an inward, experiential relationship to God and an outlook toward *sanctification that viewed the Christian life as a pilgrimage involving conflict and personal effort. The Puritans also emphasized the importance of education, the proper use of the Sabbath, engagement in *work as an aspect of one's religious vocation and familial relationships. In contrast to the connotations often associated today with the terms *puritan* or *puritanical,* the Puritans held sexual relations within marriage and *marriage itself in high regard.

Q

quietism. An approach to life that looks to God to accomplish the divine will without human attempts to act in cooperation. The term is used to denote several historical developments, most commonly a mysticism propagated in seventeenth-century Europe that held that spiritual ecstasy is attained through passive contemplation and self-emptying in the form of self-denial and withdrawal from outward activity. It also can refer to the separatist stance toward the world that came to characterize many Anabaptist groups in the wake of *persecution. In *ethics, quietism is the belief that the moral quest entails inwardness and eschews activism in the world, especially social action.

R

racism. A form of *prejudice that discriminates among persons and social groups on the basis of ethnic origin or skin color. Racism is sometimes viewed in a positive light as the appropriate separation of humans into societies based on ethnicity and is defended by appeal to supposed distinctions among the various races of humankind or to theological considerations such as God's intention that humans be separated into races. More commonly, however, racism is seen as a negative attitude, for it is generally characterized by hostility, contempt or condescension, and readily leads to social, economic and political mistreatment of others. Christians decry racism in this sense as contrary to the unity of humankind as created by God and as reconciled to God in Christ, as well as a violation of the dignity of all persons. *See also* discrimination; human dignity.

Rauschenbusch, Walter (1861-1918). A Baptist theologian considered a progenitor of the *social gospel movement in America. Rauschenbusch was acutely aware of the needs of people living in a social order that, in the wake of the industrial revolution, had become impervious to God's intentions regarding human social interaction and the just treatment of human beings. Rauschenbusch's view that biblical concepts such as *sin and the *kingdom of God are applicable to *society and that God's goal for humankind included the redemption of a sinful social order stood in stark contrast to the individual focus of the Protestant piety of the day.

Reformation ethics. The ethical stance that began with the sixteenth-century Reformers Martin Luther and Ulrich Zwingli and continued through John Calvin and the English Reformation. At the foundation of Reformation ethics is the teaching that humans are unable to please God apart from divine grace bestowed in Christ and that the ethical life arises out of the regenerating work of the Holy Spirit. Moreover, the Reformers rejected what they saw as the overly philosophical approach to ethics that characterized the medieval synthesis with its emphasis on the reasonableness of God's ethical demands (*see also* medieval ethics). The Reformers, in contrast, spoke about an inscrutable, sovereign God whose ways are higher than human reason can fathom and who commands in accordance with the divine good, pleasure and will. The proper human response to this God, in turn, is an *obedience born of *faith and the reception of God's gracious reconciliation. Reformation ethics, therefore, emphasizes the grace and *holiness of God, which is seen as demanding a personal response that leads to self-discipline, *temperance and sobriety. *See also* law, uses of; merit.

refugee. A person displaced or forced to move from one locale to another by *tyranny, harassment, *persecution, *war or any other combination of causes that have deprived him or her of home, *property, way of life or religious *freedom. Ethicists debate such issues as the causes that produce refugees, the conditions under which a person can rightly be deemed a refugee and the responsibilities of host nations toward refugees that cross their borders.

relativism. As a general concept, the assertion that all beliefs, opinions, judgments or claims to truth are conditioned by and dependent on contingent factors connected to the persons or groups that espouse them; the theory that the basis for all judgments varies according to time, place, and personal or group perspective. Hence, relativism assumes that the context in which any discourse occurs influences its outcome or the conclusions that arise from it. Relativism readily leads to the conclusion that the situational character of all discourse means either that no *absolutes or universals exist, or more narrowly that we have no access to a standpoint from which we could reach conclusions about what is absolute or universal. Moral relativism declares that assertions about the *right and the *good, as well as *laws or *principles that guide human moral behavior, are contextually conditioned. *See also* conventionalism; idealism; pluralism; postmodern ethics; universal moral judgments.

remarriage. Literally, the act of entering into a spousal relationship with a person subsequent to the severing of the *marriage covenant with another. Christian ethicists are divided as to whether *divorce entails the moral right to remarry.

remedial justice. The correction of past cases of unjust judgment. Remedial *justice is not simply correcting a process so that future occurrences do not happen, but the giving to those that were unjustly judged what was deprived of them. Hence, it entails correction and recompense for past injustices. *See also* restitution, retribution.

reproductive technologies. The various means which seek to bring the resources of technology to bear in assisting in the process of begetting human life. These methods vary from the attempt to eliminate impediments that reduce the possibility of a pregnancy occurring through normal sexual intercourse (e.g., surgical repair of blocked fallopian tubes) to the actual uniting of egg and sperm apart from intercourse (e.g., *in vitro fertilization). Other techniques enhance the likelihood of pregnancy occurring by placing either sperm (*artificial insemination) or eggs, perhaps with sperm as well (gamete intrafallopian transfer, or GIFT), in a position in the woman's body where conception might occur. *See also* procreation.

responsibility. The condition in which an individual (or perhaps a corporation or institution; *see* corporate responsibility) is subject to being called on to account or answer for something; the condition in which an agent is so related to something that the agent is deemed to be subject to certain appraisals because of that connection. Responsibility generally denotes the situation in which one is viewed as subject to blame or praise or to being judged for an attitude, deed, relationship or decision. Responsibility is often seen as encompassing both accountability and *obligation and as carrying an ethical sense. Many ethicists view responsibility as the requisite condition under which praise and blame, as well as *punishment and reward, can be placed or credited.

restitution, retribution. As used in the ethics of *punishment, these terms refer to two basic positions regarding the purpose of legal penalties imposed on civil lawbreakers. Viewed from this perspective, restitution is the repair of an injury to body, character or *property in response to an action that inflicted the injury, whereas retribution is the infliction of measured punishment in response to a specific action because such punishment is deemed to be justly deserved by the offender. In Christian teaching, however, restitution is sometimes seen as going beyond the repair of injury to include the reconciliation of the perpetrator and the victim. Christian ethicists are in general agreement that punishment ought to involve an element of restitution. They differ greatly, however, regarding the extent to which punishment ought also to be seen as retributive. The argument focuses in part on the question as to whether God's response to human sinfulness is solely directed toward restitution or also includes retribution, and whether or not God has entrusted the task of meting out retribution to human authorities or institutions. *See also* justice; penology; prison reform.

right. As an ethical term, in the adjectival sense, in accordance with what is morally sound or obligatory. A central debate in *ethics is the question as to how judgments regarding what is deemed right can be justified. *See also* justification, moral.

right to life. *See* life, right to.

righteousness. The condition of being upright, just and moral. The ancient Greeks viewed righteousness as living according to *virtue. The Bible, in contrast, applies the term primarily and fundamentally to God. The Christian tradition tends to view human righteousness initially as the condition of being put right with God as the result of divine action on humans' behalf. This new status, in turn, is intended to lead to actual righteousness in *character and conduct.

rights. The set of liberties, claims, powers, privileges and immunities to which a person has a moral, legal or just claim. In the realm of human social relationships and human societies, rights are generally divided into several types, including political rights and *civil rights, both of which are often seen as arising out of a more basic set of *human rights. In recent years, ethicists have been grappling as well with the concept of *animal rights.

robotics. The science or study of robots. Robots are mechanical devices that are designed and programmed to carry out a series of predetermined tasks. Robots are used in industries and sciences where human labor would be either too costly or too hazardous for effective production. Robotics has progressed to the point that designers are attempting to create machines with so-called artificial intelligence, which is generally seen as the ability to make autonomous decisions regarding various aspects of their tasks and perhaps even aspects of their existence. The advent of artificial intelligence raises, at least potentially, a variety of new issues, not the least of which is the moral and legal status of machines that possess a high level of intelligence. *See also* cybernetics; technological ethics.

rule-deontologism. A theory of moral reasoning within *deontological ethics that declares that the rightness or wrongness of a moral act is determined on the basis of whether it is in keeping with or violates a set of rules or moral *principles. The ethical life, in turn, consists in *obedience to such rules or principles. This position has gained adherents in both the philosophical and the Christian ethical traditions, although the two groups differ as to the source of or means to the discovery of the rules or *principles that govern *ethics. *Christian ethics appeals to the principles delineated in the Bible, whereas the philosophical tradition invokes human reason. Rule-deontologists differ with each other regarding the actual set of and even the number of governing rules or principles. *See also* hierarchicalism; principle monism.

S

Sabbatarianism. Although Sabbatarianism may be defined in a general sense as the perspective that upholds the importance of following the biblical injunction to set apart one day in seven for worship, recreation and renewal, in the history of Western ethics the term has generally been used in the more narrowly focused manner to refer to the strict adherence of Sunday or the Lord's Day as "Sabbath." Moreover, sabbatarians often advocate Sunday observance as *public policy and hence attempt to regulate Sunday activity, especially through legislation. *See also* blue laws; Sunday laws.

sanctification. Derived from the Hebrew and Greek terms meaning "to be set apart from common use," "to be made holy." Christian theology sometimes speaks of sanctification as twofold, referring first to the divine declaration that Christians have been made holy through Christ and second to the process whereby Christians are to grow into and strive for *holiness by cooperating with the indwelling Holy Spirit until they arrive at complete conformity to Christ. The concept of sanctification forms a basis for the Christian moral quest. It has also provided the impetus for several competing Christian views regarding the nature and goal of, pathway to and possibility of attaining the moral life. *See also* perfectionism.

sanctity of life. *See* life, sanctity of.

science and ethics. The relationship of science and *ethics has been a perennial question for philosophers and Christian ethicists alike. On the one hand, the discussion pursues the role that science can have in ethical reflection. Three positions are most common: science as a source of factual information upon which moral judgments are made, science as a source of values and science as a continual source of new ethical problems. The first position is loosely connected to ethical *naturalism. The second is evident in such developments as the rise of evolutionary ethics, with its assertion that the scientific fact of evolution leads to the concept of progress as a moral ideal. The third attitude has been abetted by the plethora of discoveries in such areas as *genetics, *nuclear energy and military technology that have raised widespread concern. On the other hand, the discussion regarding ethics and science explores the moral basis of the scientific enterprise itself, including such issues as the extent to which scientific inquiry as an aspect of the human quest for knowledge is an absolute right. In this context, ethicists express concern about the growing sense that science and technology are morally self-justifying. *See also* experimentation; secularization; technological ethics.

secularization. The process by which a religiously informed view of the universe, social relationships and personal existence is displaced by an outlook that seeks to make sense out of the world without appeal to beliefs about God or what lies beyond the universe itself. The secularization process is abetted by the assumption that the methods of empirical science are capable of discovering all that is real, or that the scientific method provides our only access to what may legitimately be deemed real, meaningful or of value (*see also* science and ethics). Furthermore, values that arise out of religious traditions are dismissed or deemed inadmissible in the process of framing *public policy and determining the moral *norms of the *society. Secularization not only fosters the disaffection of religion from society, it also dilutes the normative role of traditional sources of authority within a religious *community.

Sermon on the Mount. The series of teachings by Jesus, found in the First Gospel (in Matthew 5—7) and considered by Christians to comprise the heart of his moral perspective, especially as it constitutes his reiteration and reinterpretation of the Old Testament *law. The Sermon on the Mount sets forth the way of life for the Christian disciple and the Christian *community. In Western culture, the Sermon on the Mount has been consistently hailed as the epitome of high moral *idealism. In the Christian tradition, the Sermon on the Mount has been seen alternatively as a set of general moral *principles loosely applicable to various contexts and as the blueprint for a particular and radical life of discipleship. More recently, the christological and eschatological character of Jesus' ethic in general and the Sermon on the Mount in particular has come to the fore (*see also* eschatology, its role in ethics). Insofar as Jesus himself is the fulfillment of what God's law demands, the appropriation of Jesus' work by *faith and the indwelling presence of the Holy Spirit enables the practical *obedience to the ethic that the Sermon on the Mount enjoins. *See also* golden rule; Jesus, ethic of; New Testament ethics.

seven deadly sins. A list of sins, compiled at various times in the Christian tradition, that are singled out for special note in that they are believed to be the gateway to other sins. These sins are generally enumerated as pride, envy, anger, *sloth, *greed, *gluttony and *lust. *See also* vice.

sexuality, sexual ethics. Sexuality may be defined broadly as the various dimensions of human existence that are connected to our condition as sexual beings or to our being embodied creatures who are either male or female. Sexuality is often used more narrowly to refer to the various ways in which humans express their sexuality in acts or behaviors, especially as these behaviors involve the human sex organs. Sexual ethics, in turn is the study of the moral framework that pertains to human sexuality, the application of moral considerations to human sexual relationships. As a course of study, sexual ethics explores a variety of issues of personal or social conduct, such as the proper context of sexual intercourse, the morality of *masturbation, the nature of *marriage and the marital covenant, the propriety of *divorce and *remarriage, the moral status of *birth control and *reproductive technologies and their place in *procreation, and the ethical standing of sexual practices that are often deemed aberrant, illegal or detrimental to personal or social well-being. Recent years have witnessed an increase in the topics discussed under the purview of sexual ethics, as is evident, for example, in the question of the ethics of *virtual sex. Christian sexual ethics seeks to elucidate these questions from the perspective of God's intention for human existence as sexual creatures. *See also* homosexuality; pederasty, pedophilia.

shame. The feeling of psychological pain that follows or is experienced when a person realizes that an act has been committed that does not live up to ideals or expectations; the sense of discomfort that arises in the wake of a sensed failure. Shame can be felt on behalf of oneself, of another person or a group. As an ethical term, shame is the sense of moral discomfort arising from a failure that is deemed sinful, such as an act that violates a known moral standard. Viewed from the ethical perspective, shame may be seen as the sense of moral guilt. Shame and *guilt are not synonymous, however, in that the latter carries objective connotations as well as (possibly) including a subjective sense, whereas shame is best seen as limited to the subjective feeling itself.

simony. The practice of buying or selling ecclesiastical favor or sacred prerogatives. The term is derived from Simon Magus, who attempted to purchase the ability to bestow the Holy Spirit through the act of laying on of hands, and thus sought to buy spiritual prerogatives or perhaps apostolic authority with money (Acts 8:9-13, 18-24).

sin. A general Christian theological concept denoting the fundamental unbelief, distrust and rejection of God, or the denial of God's rightful place as sovereign over creation in general, and as sovereign over one's own life and relationships. Sin is both the state of separation and alienation from God that characterizes fallen humankind, and purposeful disobedience to God's will as evidenced in concrete thought or act. The latter reflects the manner in which the term is generally used in *ethics. Sin is a disposition or an act that is contrary to what ought either to characterize a person or be done by a person. Sin is often used to refer to a deliberate violation of a moral boundary, although an ignorant transgression is also technically a sin. Not only the nature of sin but also its source (e.g., whether it arises out of a particular aspect of personal existence, whether it is largely the result of social conditioning, etc.) are perennial topics of discussion in ethics. *See also* crime; guilt; mortal sin; original sin.

situation ethics. A term coined by the Episcopalian theologian Joseph Fletcher to denote the ethical theory that *love is the primary, if not the only, *principle governing moral action, and consequently that all other ethical principles and *laws are illuminative, rather than descriptive, in nature and force. Situation ethics is situational in that it assumes that the form that the principle of love will take in any particular circumstance cannot be determined by abstract reflection prior to or apart from the situation itself. Thus, situation ethics teaches that in any given situation the moral agent must seek to discern what in that circumstance would be the most loving course of action and then act accordingly.

slander. The act of uttering false statements, or disseminating misinformation, for the purpose of defaming or injuring the reputation of another person. Technically, slander occurs when the defamatory statement is articulated in a transient form such as audible speech. When the form is more permanent, such as in writing or a public broadcast, it becomes libel, and thus potentially a criminal offense.

slavery. A form of servitude in which a human being becomes the property and serves the economic advantage of others. Slavery was common in ancient societies. The Bible frequently refers to the institution of slavery and provides injunctions regarding the proper attitude toward and treatment of slaves, as well as the relationship between master and slave in a manner that has come to be seen as undermining the entire practice. Under the influence of the Christian faith, slavery came to an end in Europe in 1815 and in the United States with the Emancipation Proclamation (1863) and the Thirteenth Amendment (1865), which came in the wake of the Civil War (1861-1865). Slavery is considered morally repugnant because it reduces a human person to the status of property, thereby violating the slave's *human rights and dehumanizing both master and slave. Moreover, the Christian perspective suggests that slavery abrogates to a human what properly belongs only to God, namely, the divine prerogative as Lord.

slippery slope. An argument that cautions against an action that may not necessarily be objectionable in itself on the basis that it would set in motion a train of events that would lead to an undesirable outcome. The slippery slope argument has been used in the debates over several contemporary ethical issues. For example, some ethicists argue against legalizing voluntary *euthanasia because it will lead to such evils as the imposition of social expectations on elderly or terminally ill persons to end their lives prematurely or that it will open the door to *involuntary euthanasia.

sloth. A *vice characterized by a disinclination to exertion, by laziness or by the lack of zeal. Sloth is viewed as a vice in both ancient Greek and *Christian ethics. In the Christian tradition, sloth has been numbered as one of the *seven deadly sins, and it often assumes spiritual overtones, such as in *Thomas Aquinas's description of sloth as spiritual apathy.

social ethics. Ethical reflection that focuses on societal structures and processes and on how particular social contexts shape *morality. Social ethics also explores the ethical dimensions of and ethical problems that arise in the workings of social structures, including government, as well as such aspects of the human social reality as economic life, international policy and the dynamics within communities. In that it looks at the ethical aspects of humans in relationship, social ethics is often contrasted with *personal ethics. Insofar as human beings are by nature social, there is a sense that all ethical reflection must be social, for *ethics must invariably take seriously the sociality of human existence. *See also* economic system; international order; politics.

social gospel. An approach to the Christian faith, popularized by Walter *Rauschenbusch early in the twentieth century, that emphasizes the social implications of the gospel and calls the church to give attention to social action on the basis of the theological vision of the *kingdom of God. Proponents of the social gospel assert that the Christian task includes partnering with God in transforming human *society along the lines of the kingdom of God, a goal advanced by means of the regeneration of all human relationships. Social gospel advocates call on Christians to work for the transformation of economic structures that perpetuate *poverty and injustice. *See also* liberation ethics; social justice.

social justice. As the application of the more general category of *justice to a central dimension of human existence, social justice focuses on the *common good of the *community as it is manifested in such areas as the fair and equal distribution of goods and benefits, as well as in respect for the *rights of others. *See also* distributive justice.

socialism. An idealist vision for the fostering of *equality, *justice, *freedom and *fairness in *society that sees as the means to this goal the common control or ownership of revenue-bearing properties and the means of production, as well as centralized management or directing of the economic processes. According to socialism, equality is the basic value, and as a consequence justifies coercion insofar as it promotes equality. Ethicists have debated the relative merits of socialism and capitalism as economic theories. Christian ethicists have engaged in a similar conversation, generally, however, raising the question as to which theory better fits with biblical teaching or better reflects the concerns of the gospel. As a political ideology and economic theory, socialism is often used interchangeably with communism and *Marxism. *See also* economic system; welfare state.

society. A group of people in interdependent relationships with each other and whose relationships are governed by *custom, convention or perhaps *law, especially insofar as they interact with each other because of some link such as a geographical location. A society may likewise be characterized by a common language, culture and values. Some theorists draw a distinction between a society, which is viewed as utilitarian, impersonal, economic and political in orientation, and a *community, which is seen to be more personal and oriented toward common values.

Socrates (470-400 B.C.), Socratic ethics. An ancient Greek philosopher, the teacher of *Plato, who is known to the contemporary world only through his pupil's representation of him. He was likely born in Athens, where he spent most of his life. He engaged in a philosophical method that contrasted sharply with the Sophists, which, in turn, likely led to his trial and conviction by the Athenians. His guiding dictum was that the only life worth living was the examined life, a view that led to the Socratic admonition, "Know yourself." Socrates drew a close connection between knowledge and *virtue, insofar as he postulated that no one does *evil knowingly, but chooses it only if in the moment it is mistaken for a *good. He also taught—and this led to his willingness to drink the poison to which he was sentenced—that it is always better to suffer than to do evil. This led to the idea that insofar as the inner life can be strengthened through right conduct, the ethical life is connected to the soul.

sodomy. A term generally denoting male homosexual intercourse, usually through anal penetration. The derivation of the word from the Old Testament city of Sodom, which was destroyed for its wickedness (Gen 19:1-28), indicates the degree to which such acts were often deemed despicable in the Christian tradition. *See also* homosexuality.

standards. The ethical *norms that serve to define the nature of obligatory and permitted actions, or to guide human beings toward *right and away from wrong behaviors. Moral standards may also designate the general understandings of what constitutes decent or morally admissible behavior that characterize a particular *society.

sterilization. The procedure by which a human being or an animal is rendered incapable of reproducing sexually. It is generally accomplished in females by tubal ligation, that is, severing the fallopian tubs, whereas in males it takes the form of vasectomy, i.e., the severing of the sperm ducts. Sterilization may be either voluntary or nonvoluntary. Its purpose may be contraceptive, therapeutic or punitive. In part due to the influence from proponents of *eugenics, forced sterilization was practiced in both the United States and Canada throughout the first half of the twentieth century. Such practices are strongly opposed by many ethicists today. The use of sterilization as a permanent means of contraceptive is now widely practiced, but is also ethically controversial. Apart from the question of the *morality of *contraception in general, critics find its invasive and permanent nature morally unacceptable. *See also* procreation.

stewardship. The *principle that declares that the proper ethical stance begins with the acknowledgment of God as the owner of everything in creation, and as a consequence views human beings as responsible to God for the wise use of all that is entrusted to them to administer in a manner in keeping with God's intended purposes. Often stewardship is viewed in the narrow sense of a person's *responsibility for one's material resources, especially money and possessions. In this sense, the principle of being responsible to God extends to the various aspects of one's financial dealings: earning, spending, buying, saving, investing and giving. Today, stewardship is generally understood in a more holistic or all-inclusive sense. The human managerial responsibility extends to all areas of life, both individual and communal, and includes both attitude and action. Stewardship as a spiritual principle is taught in the Bible. Moreover, many Christian ethicists see it as directly applicable to current issues ranging from *economic systems to *ecology.

Stoics, Stoic ethics. The Stoics, derived from the Greek *stoa poikilē*, the designation of the pointed porch in Athens where the philosophers gathered, were a group of thinkers whose teachings were widely followed in the ancient first-century world. According to the Stoics, the ultimate goal of life is *wisdom, understood as living according to *nature, that is, allowing human reason—as the connecting point with the divine reason that permeates the universe—to govern one's life. Hence, for the Stoics, *ethics was the central concern of philosophy. Their understanding of the ethical life, in turn, was connected to a fatalistic conception that viewed every event as the product of the divine will or providence. Because human assent or *will is the one thing in the universe that escapes *determinism, virtue involves conscious assent to the inevitable order of things. In this understanding of *virtue, the Stoics pitted reason against the desires and emotions, which they saw as irrational. Virtue consists of controlling our reactions or practicing self-control. Above all, the virtuous person keeps the emotions in check. The Stoic expresses neither joy nor sorrow, regardless of the outward circumstances. According to the New Testament, Paul engaged directly with the Stoic philosophers in Athens (Acts 17:18), and his epistles sometimes draw from Stoic themes. The Stoics also influenced *Christian ethics in the patristic era (*see also* patristic ethics).

suffering. The condition of enduring a series events that are physically and emotionally undesirable, or the experience of anguish and misery connected with that condition. Various suggestions have been proposed regarding the source, purpose and means of overcoming suffering. The biblical writers indicate that suffering is somehow connected to *sin and the fall. This leads some to the half-truth that suffering arises as a *punishment for personal sins or wrong actions. The New Testament declares that Christ's death marks the act of God shouldering the suffering of creation. As a consequence, suffering can contribute to *character development and can be a way of sharing in Christ's great self-giving act on the cross. Most Christian ethicists see Christ's mandate as including the task of ministering to those who are suffering and seeking to alleviate the causes of suffering.

suicide. The deliberate termination of one's own life. Whereas some ancient Greek philosophers, such as Seneca, defended the right to commit suicide as a corollary of human *freedom, the Christian tradition, with only a few exceptions, has viewed the act as morally wrong both because it constitutes *murder and because it violates divine providence and divine sovereignty over human life. In recent years, the *euthanasia debate has reopened the question of suicide, especially with respect to terminally ill persons. One aspect of this question is the matter of "doctor assisted suicide," that is, the idea that a terminally ill person should be able to end his or her life by means of taking a lethal dose of some drug with the aid of a physician.

summum bonum. A Latin term that means literally "highest good." In ethical theory, the good in relation to which all other values are ordered, or in accordance to which all other values are measured. *See also* good, goodness; good life.

sumptuary laws. Legislation intended to restrain excessive or lavish expenditures, generally for the sake of preventing extravagant living.

Sunday laws. A series of legal statutes, originally intended to promote the observance of Sunday as a holy day or a day of worship, that prohibited forms of entertainment and the conduct of business on Sunday. Although governments are less likely today to enact such legislation on the basis of worship preferences of Christians, some ethicists argue for a continuation of such laws as a way not only of fostering just treatment of workers and business *employees, but also of insuring that small, family-run businesses are able to compete favorably with larger companies. *See also* blue laws; Sabbatarianism.

superego. *See* id, ego, superego.

supererogation, acts of. Going beyond the call of *duty. As a term in Roman Catholic Church teaching, supererogation denotes the performance of *good works that *merit more than personal salvation. As an ethical term, supererogatory acts are either acts that *morality encourages but not does not require, or acts that indicate a superior moral *character. Giving to *charity is an example of the first use of the term, whereas acts that are especially saintly or heroic would qualify for the second sense of this designation. Acts of supererogation are deemed praiseworthy, but their omission does not invoke blame. Some ethicists deny the possibility of such acts ever being performed. In a *deontological ethics framework, our duty may be viewed as so all-encompassing as to make the possibility of going beyond duty impossible. Similarly, a consequentialist understanding (*see* teleological ethics) might declare that a person is always required to act so as to bring about the greatest amount of *good possible. Or it might be argued that God demands that we do our best in every situation.

swearing. Used in two basic ways: First, swearing is the invoking of a divine name or divine imagery as a means of validating one's pledge. The common practice of a witness voicing an oath prior to giving testimony in a courtroom is an example of this use. Second, swearing can denote the practice of invoking the name of God "in vain," that is, disingenuously or profanely, in common speech. This practice is often decried in that it debases the use of language. *Christian ethics tends to see a more ethically repugnant dimension in it, for it is not only a corruption of sacred language, but it also violates the biblical injunction to hallow the divine name (e.g., Ex 20:7). In general, Christian ethicists have supported the practice of swearing in the first sense, although some Christian groups (e.g., Anabaptists) reject it as a transgression of Jesus' instructions in the *Sermon on the Mount (Mt 5:33-37).

sympathy. The condition of being in agreement in feeling with another or others; the ability to understand or to share the feelings of others. Sympathy is closely connected to *compassion, and is generally viewed as the underlying ability that makes compassion possible.

synderesis. Deemed by some to be derived from the Greek word *syneidēsis,* meaning "conscience," but by others as arising from *syntērēsis* ("guard closely"), the term used by medieval theologians to designate a knowledge of the first *principles of moral action. Although some medievalists equated synderesis with *conscience, *Thomas Aquinas differentiated the two, seeing the former as the grasp of moral principles and the latter as the application of this knowledge to specific circumstances.

T

taboo. A prohibition enforced by the threat of reason-defying catastrophe or supernaturally induced consequences that will come to the transgressor or perhaps extend to his or her *family, relatives or the entire *community. The object of a taboo is often viewed as invested with strong power. The term is borrowed from South Pacific Polynesian cultures. In common Western usage, taboo refers to anything forbidden by general societal prohibition.

technical virginity. In popular parlance, the situation in which a person can claim to be a virgin, even though she or he has engaged in a variety of sexual acts or behaviors, because those behaviors have not included actual sexual intercourse. The term often arises when unmarried persons who believe that sexual intercourse outside of (i.e., prior to) *marriage is sinful are attempting to establish moral limits for their sexual activity. Viewed from a Christian perspective, the term fails to reflect a full awareness of the purpose of sexual foreplay nor of the biblical perspective on the purpose of human sexuality. *See also* chastity; sexuality, sexual ethics.

technological ethics. The study of the implications of technology in general or of specific technologies for moral behavior, as well as the application of moral *principles to the use of technology. As a field of study, technological ethics first emerged on a large scale in the nineteenth century in response to the Industrial Revolution (*see also* industrial ethics). Recent technological developments have triggered ethical discussions regarding the use of such technologies as nuclear weapons and power (*see* nuclear energy; nuclear warfare), chemical fertilizers and defoliants (*see also* ecology), genetic engineering (*see* genetics), and *cloning. In addition, ethicists explore such overarching questions as: Is technology morally neutral? How does technology reshape human values? What constitutes responsible technology? In response to the first question, some ethicists assert that technology is neutral and that the moral questions all lie in the area of its use. Others, in contrast, aver that technology is itself value-laden.

teleological ethics. An approach to moral reasoning, sometimes known as consequentialism, that asserts that the rightness or wrongness of an act is determined by its outcome, namely, by the amount of *good it produces or *evil it prevents. Hence, in any given situation the moral agent should inquire as to which act will produce the greatest possible balance of good over evil. Proponents of the teleological approach differ with each other regarding whose benefit ought to be the concern of the moral agent, some arguing that one's own good is the sole concern (*ethical egoism), whereas others aver that the good of others must be considered (*utilitarianism).

temperance. As an ethical term, temperance is used in two ways. First, the term denotes a *virtue prevalent in both Greek and Christian ethical thought that is associated with moderation and self-control, especially with respect to desires and appetites. The word itself is related to the Greek term *sōphrosunē,* which suggests the restraint of desires and the mastery of passions. *Plato considered temperance as one of the four *cardinal virtues and spoke of it as the virtue of self-control. He described temperance as the use of reason and *will in the mastery of the appetites and the passions. *Thomas Aquinas viewed temperance as both a general and specific virtue. In the former sense, it moderates the other moral virtues, whereas in the latter it controls the bodily pleasures. Hence, temperance was to be associated with proportion and moral discernment. Second, temperance refers to a late nineteenth- and early twentieth-century social movement that advocated the moderate use of or, for some proponents, the total abstinence from the consumption of alcoholic beverages.

temptation. That which attempts to persuade a person to do wrong, especially by promising a *good result such as *pleasure or gain; the condition of being attracted to a course of action that is inappropriate or inconsistent with one's religious or moral beliefs. The concept of temptation is prevalent throughout the Bible, which portrays the source of the enticement to do wrong as a supernatural *evil force (*sin) or being (Satan) or as a disposition within the human person (e.g., the *flesh or the fallen nature). However, temptation can also denote a testing, often with the goal of bringing a person to a higher level of knowing, honoring or serving God.

terrorism. The use of armed violence, both militaristic and nonmilitaristic, in such a manner as to produce terror in a populace and consequently achieve specific political aims. Intentionally, terrorism attacks civilian targets in order to create a climate of fear and anxiety in order to achieve its ends. Terrorism arises from a variety of sources, such as religious fanaticism, economic privation and political corruption. Unpredictable methodology, random target selection and a complete disrespect for the ethical conduct adhered to in declared *war (e.g., the Geneva Convention) mark terrorism. As a manner of warfare, terrorism has been practiced from the earliest of times. In the New Testament period, the Zealots, according to their methodology, were considered terrorists. Theologians and political theorists continue to debate whether there is ever any circumstance in which terrorism is ethical.

test tube babies. A popular designation for children produced by the *reproductive technologies of *in vitro fertilization and embryonic transfer. In these processes, egg and sperm are combined in the laboratory to produce a human *zygote, which is then transplanted to a host womb for development.

theological virtues. The set of *virtues that are rooted in the character of God and cannot be attained by means of human effort or through the application of human ability alone, but require the infusion of divine grace; the virtues of the Christian life that must be bestowed by God. The concept of the theological virtues is derived from Paul's elevation of *faith, hope and *love as abiding eternally and therefore as ranking above those characteristics of the Christian life that are merely temporal (1 Cor 13:13). Consequently, the theological virtues are generally contrasted with the natural virtues enumerated in the Greek philosophical tradition, especially the *cardinal virtues of *wisdom, *courage, *temperance and *justice. By the fourteenth century, the two classes came to be combined as the seven cardinal virtues and contrasted with the *seven deadly sins.

theological voluntarism. The teaching that moral *standards arise solely from the divine will, or that the sole or ultimate standard for *right and wrong is the divine will. Adherents of this position suggest that the divine will can be known, insofar as God reveals it to humans. God's will is often believed to be expressed in the law of God. *See also* metaphysical moralism; theonomy.

theonomy. The condition of living under divine rule; as an ethical term, the belief that God is ultimate source of moral authority, and hence that revelation, rather than reason, is the central locus for ethical guidance. Under this broader meaning, theonomy can denote a variety of ethical proposals, although it is most often used to refer to *theological voluntarism, i.e., the teaching that moral *standards arise solely from the divine will, in contrast to *naturalism or the idea that ethical *norms are inherent in the *nature of things. Recently, theonomy has been used to denote a political movement, sometimes called reconstructionism, that advocates a kind of theocracy in which the revealed divine law, including the laws of the Old Testament, becomes the legislated law of the nation. Theonomy can also denote an approach to *Christian ethics that attempts to set forth a position between *autonomy and *heteronomy by integrating the two authorities of the written word and the Spirit. The foundational assumption of theonomy, viewed from this perspective, is that humans live in relationship, primarily to God and secondarily to other humans as well as creation. The goal of ethical reflection, in turn, is to discern from the biblical vision of God's purposes for human existence what it means to live with *integrity in each particular context of one's life.

Thomas Aquinas (1225-1274). A medieval Italian theologian and monk whose work was declared to be the official teaching of the Roman Catholic Church by Pope Leo XIII in 1879. Thomas was best known for his *Summa Theologica,* a systematic presentation of Christian theology based on the work of *Aristotle. In the realm of *ethics, Thomas is credited with placing ethics within the context of the *telos* or goal of existence. He begins with the Aristotelian insight that agents always act with a specific end in view. This belief leads to the assertion that the *telos* of any existing thing is good, with the highest *good and the fountain of all goodness being God. Therefore, the human movement towards its *telos,* the highest good, or God, stands at the heart of his ethics. *See also* teleological ethics.

Thomistic ethics. The ethical theory proposed by *Thomas Aquinas or the tradition of ethical reflection that has its origin in his writings. Although he was a highly controversial thinker in his own day, his legacy in Western—especially Roman Catholic—theological and ethical thought is perhaps second only to *Augustine. The first impulse leading to Thomism as a specific tradition centers around the thinkers who followed Thomas's lead, often at great personal cost, during the first half-century following his death in 1274. A second period in which Thomism flourished was during the sixteenth and seventeenth centuries, an era known as Second Thomism. After a period of neglect, Thomism underwent a revival and rethinking during the late nineteenth and twentieth centuries, especially under the leadership of a group of thinkers known as the Neo-Thomists. Thomistic ethics are teleological in orientation, emphasizing that human beings have a natural desire for the perfect good—God—as their ultimate end. It is to this end that all human good must be conformed. It follows that a good life consists in the use of intellect, will and sense, under the control of right reason, in the cultivation of virtuous habits that are either attained by practice or infused by God. *See also* cardinal virtues; synderesis; teleological ethics.

tolerance, toleration. Narrowly defined, as an ethical term, tolerance is the quality of being long-suffering in disposition; the putting up with something with which one disagrees. The verb, *tolerate,* means to allow without opposing; to acknowledge the right of another to hold contrary opinions. Toleration, in turn, is the condition in which beliefs or behaviors—especially religious or political—that do not conform to that of the majority or dominant group in a *society are allowed to be present and perhaps propagated without opposition in the form of legislation or the use of *force. Toleration did not emerge as a *public policy ideal until after the Reformation. Moreover, toleration assumes the dominance of one particular viewpoint. Hence, religious toleration—in contrast to religious liberty—maintains an established church while allowing the existence of dissenting ecclesial groups. Beginning in the late twentieth century, tolerance was elevated as a cardinal *virtue, although it is sometimes understood to denote a kind of moral *relativism, which transforms it into the disposition that not only allows contrary positions, but deems all opinions (including one's own) to be equally valid. *See also* pluralism.

total depravity. A theological teaching, generally linked to *Augustine and especially the followers of Calvin, that the condition of *sin has rendered humankind so helpless that no one is able to obtain salvation through personal effort. The doctrine declares as well that the effects of the fall extend to every dimension of human existence, so that we dare not place complete trust in any human ability (such as reason). This aspect of total depravity was a central aspect of the Reformers' critique of the ethical system of the medieval Roman Catholic Church. *See also* Reformation ethics.

totalitarianism. The political theory that invests the state with the right to exercise oversight or even control over all aspects of the lives of its citizens. The term was first put forward by Mussolini in describing the Fascist state as *stato totalitario.* Totalitarianism has been criticized by ethicists in general as being incompatible with the idea that the human person is the entity in whom *rights are ultimately invested and by Christian ethicists as usurping for the state prerogatives that belong solely to God.

totality principle. A *principle of *morality that states that the *good of a part may be sacrificed for the good of the whole. This principle has been used in *medical ethics to justify certain medical procedures that remove a part of the body in order to save the whole. Insofar as the totality principle appears to be a restatement of *utilitarianism and has been associated with the dictum "the ends justify the means," it is rejected by those ethicists who follow the approach to moral reasoning of *deontological ethics.

trait-deontologism. A deontological theory of moral reasoning, connected to the broader approach known as the *ethic of being, that declares that certain character traits are intrinsically *good and therefore that the moral life consists of developing these *virtues. *See also* deontological ethics.

trait-egoism. A variety of *trait-teleologism that declares that the moral value of any character trait is determined by the amount of *good or *evil that results for the moral agent who possesses it. The moral life, therefore, consists of cultivating those traits that are most conducive to one's own welfare. *See also* ethical egoism.

trait-teleologism. A category of theories of moral reasoning, connected to the broader approach known as the *ethic of being, that declares that the value of a character trait is determined by the *good or *evil that results from their presence in a moral agent. The moral life, therefore, consists of the development of the traits that produce good rather than evil results. *See also* teleological ethics.

trait-utilitarianism. A variety of *trait-teleologism that declares that the moral value of any character trait is determined by the amount of *good or *evil that its presence in a moral agent produces in the world as a whole. The moral life, therefore, consists of cultivating those traits that are most conducive to the welfare of all others or that promote the general good. *See also* utilitarianism.

transplants. *See* organ transplants.

transsexual. A person who is physiologically of one sex but who experiences his or her sexuality as a member of the other sex. Transsexual persons often speak of their experience as that of being "trapped in the wrong body." The condition has been known from early antiquity and is evidenced in various cultures. Transsexualism is to be differentiated from such conditions as hermaphroditism, transvestism and *homosexuality. Transsexuality is sometimes treated by a medical procedure (a sex change operation) designed to alter people's physical features and sexual characteristics so that their physiology matches their psychological gender. The procedure has ignited a debate between those who see it as a way of correcting a malady and those who claim that it violates the person's God-given (or natural) and hence unalterable status as male or female.

tyranny, tyrannicide. Tyranny is a political situation in which a people or nation are subject to cruel and oppressive rule, whether by a single governor or by a group. Although as it is used today tyranny almost always carries negative connotations, the ancient Greek term *turannos* simply referred to one who seizes *power. Tyrannicide denotes the act of removing a tyrant from power by means of assassination. Since ancient times, ethicists have debated the question as to whether or not tyrannicide is morally justifiable. Examples of the practice are found in the Old Testament (e.g., Judg 3:15-30; 2 Kings 9:21-37). It was condoned or even viewed as a positive moral *duty by several Greek philosophers and Christian thinkers. However, apart from the broader issue as to whether killing is ever justified, tyrannicide raises questions as to the point at which a ruler is no longer fit to rule, who is authorized to make such a determination, and who is invested with the prerogative of carrying out the assassination. In the twentieth century the issue surfaced in *Christian ethics in a poignant manner, when Dietrich Bonhoeffer's personal struggles with the tyrannical rule of Hitler came to light.

U

universal moral judgments, universalizability. Universal moral judgments are those assertions deemed applicable in all situations. The existence of universal moral judgments has been widely acknowledged in the Western ethical tradition, although the idea has always been controversial and is questioned today by advocates of such alternative perspectives as *relativism. Some ethicists link moral universals to what is known as the principle of universality or the universalizability axiom, which is generally viewed as merely a restatement of *Kant's first formulation of the *categorical imperative. In this understanding, a maxim or moral *principle that one would will to be a universal law is deemed by that person to be universalizable and hence morally applicable, whereas any maxim that is not universalizable in this sense does not denote what is one's *duty. Another formulation of the universalizability axiom asserts, "What is *right (or wrong) for a particular person is right (or wrong) for any similar person in all similar circumstances."

usury. Originally, the act or practice of lending money at interest. Today the term is generally used to refer to the act of charging interest that is excessive or unlawfully high. Usury in the original sense of the word was widely condemned until the modern era.

The Old Testament viewed accepting interest on a loan as sinful (e.g., Prov 28:8 NASB, RSV), and Jesus urged his followers to lend to others freely (Lk 6:34-35), largely because loans were not intended to provide temporary capital for a business venture but to sustain the very life of a poor person.

utilitarianism. A theory of moral reasoning within *teleological ethics that looks to the principle of utility, that is, the degree to which an act is helpful or harmful in the world as a whole, to determine the rightness or wrongness of an act. Moral living, therefore, consists in doing that act that brings about the greatest balance of *good over *evil for the greatest number of people.

V

value judgment. An assertion that expresses what one values (or perhaps that articulates a standard of value); a declaration that ascribes worth or *goodness to an object, including a person, a character trait or a state of being. In *ethics, value judgments may be contrasted with judgments of *obligation, which are assertions regarding what one ought to do or be. One task of ethics is to develop a normative theory of value. *See also* intrinsic value; hedonism; judgments, types of; normative ethics.

venial sin. *See* mortal sin.

vice. As an ethical term, an inner disposition to perform morally wrong acts of a certain kind; a tendency to *sin habitually in a particular manner; a character trait that is deemed blameworthy. Like *virtues, vices are associated primarily with the inner disposition to act in a certain manner and not with the acts themselves, although this distinction is not always evident in popular ethical discourse. The "cardinal" vices are sometimes listed together as the *seven deadly sins. *See also* character.

virginity, technical. *See* technical virginity.

virtual sex. The fabrication of sexual activity through the use of audio and visual stimulation, usually in the form of electronic media, without actual physical contact with the other person(s) involved. Some ethicists hail the advent of virtual sex as a means for providing a technological alternative to such social ills as *prostitution and as decreasing the ill side effects of sexual promiscuity, including unintended pregnancy and the spread of venereal diseases. Virtual sex is also seen as having potential therapeutic uses in cases of persons suffering from certain psychological and sexual disorders. Other ethicists aver that virtual sex is yet another outworking of a sexually permissive social climate and that its potential for *evil outweighs any possible *good that it might bring. *See also* sexuality, sexual ethics.

virtue. As an ethical term, an inner disposition to perform morally *right acts of a certain kind; a tendency to act rightly by *habit in a particular manner; a character trait that is deemed morally praiseworthy. The virtues have also been understood to be those qualities of *character that make a person morally successful. Ethicists in both the Greek and Christian moral traditions have sought to determine what traits are virtues. The efforts of the Greek philosophers have sometimes been summarized by reference to the four *cardinal virtues, generally enumerated as *wisdom or *prudence, *courage or *fortitude, *temperance, and *justice. To this list, *Christian ethics sometimes adds the three *theological virtues: *faith, hope and *love. Recent years have witnessed a renewed interest in the virtues, especially with the renaissance in virtue ethics or the *ethic of being.

volition. *See* will.

W

war. Armed conflict between nations or people groups. War is sometimes also used in a metaphorical sense to refer to any protracted struggle between people or forces, or a state of conflict directed against a foe of any type. The question of the justifiability of war in the form of armed conflict has been a perennial topic in *ethics. In the Christian tradition, ethicists have tended to gravitate to two opposing views: the *just war theory and *pacifism or its variants such as *nonviolence. Some ethicists aver that the advent of *nuclear warfare has drastically altered the face of the traditional discussion. *See also* biological warfare; terrorism.

wealth. As an economic term, the accumulation and ownership of an abundance of money, goods, possessions and *property. Wealth is also used in a broader sense of the abundance of anything, whether material or intangible. Such matters as the means employed in the accumulation of wealth, the use of wealth and even the actual possession of wealth have triggered ethical reflection. Regarding the latter, ethicists have historically been divided between those who view the possession of an abundance as morally problematic—some to the point of asserting that the pathway to the moral life includes divesting oneself of all earthly possessions and taking a vow of *poverty—and those who see wealth either as neutral or as a sign of personal *virtue, personal *righteousness or even the favor God.

welfare state. A social system in which the government assumes much, if not complete, *responsibility for the economic well-being of its citizens. In a welfare state, not only such matters as public transportation, utilities and postal service, but also higher education, *health care, retirement pensions and a variety of insurance programs might either be regulated or managed by the government, sometimes even to the point of being funded through government subsidy and considered entitlements for its citizens. *See also* socialism.

whistle-blowing. A metaphor, derived from the act of sounding an alarm, that denotes the act of reporting to the proper authority a behavior or a situation deemed grossly unethical or a serious problem requiring immediate correction. Whistle-blowing is generally used with reference to gross violations of protocol, morally repugnant activity, or illegal practices—such as fraud or corruption—on the part of persons within agencies, corporations or institutions that in some sense hold the public trust. Moreover, the person who discloses the situation is generally someone within the agency, corporation or institution and therefore is privy to inside information that can substantiate the claim of impropriety. Whistle-blowing usually occurs when the person has exhausted all other means of redress. Although whistle-blowing is generally viewed as *right or perhaps even enjoined as a moral *duty, ethicists debate the conditions under which it may properly occur, as well as the kind of motivation that must be displayed for the act to be laudable.

will. As a philosophical and ethical concept, the will or the volition has been defined in various ways. The basic idea is that the will is the power of an individual to make conscious, deliberate choices or to act in a deliberate manner. The Greek philosophers viewed the will as a faculty in the mind, closely associated with but not identical to reason. The will was seen as the disposition of the mind to action, preferably in accordance with reason. Today, the will tends to be understood not so much as a separate mental faculty but as the whole person behaving in specific ways for the purpose of bringing about some state of affairs. In this understanding, the will not only inaugurates an act but also continues through it. One perplexing problem in philosophy, theology and *ethics is that of the relationship of the will to motives, which in turn leads to the debate over *free will.

wisdom. A character trait, universally acknowledged as a *virtue, that is generally associated with the ability to live well in the sense of being a moral and exemplary human. It is sometimes defined as the ability to make sound judgments regarding what ought to be done or how one ought to act on the basis of a prior discernment of what is true, *right and *good. In Greek thought, wisdom, as one of the *cardinal virtues, is connected to the intellect or reason. *Aristotle differentiated between theoretical wisdom (the ability to grasp the nature of reality) and practical wisdom (the ability to make sound judgments regarding proper conduct). Christian ethicists have often described wisdom as knowing the proper way to live and then applying such knowledge so as to live properly.

work. In its basic sense, work refers to the expenditure of energy in continued physical or mental activity that is directed toward some purpose. More specifically, as a concept for ethical reflection, it is the condition of engaging in some particular activity or series of activities deemed needful, with the expectation of receiving a tangible or intangible reward (*see also* employment). In this sense, work is often contrasted with both rest and play. Work that emanates from or requires specific training or a specific calling is often termed a vocation. Many of the Greek philosophers viewed work as less lofty than the life of contemplation, a perspective that greatly influenced Christian thought at least until the Reformation. The Bible, in contrast, places work in the context of God's intentions for human existence. The Reformers set forth an understanding of work that extended the concept of vocation—which in the Middle Ages had been reserved to denote the clerical or monastic callings—to all legitimate areas of human effort (*see also* Reformation ethics). Today, many theorists advocate a utilitarian understanding that suggests that the value of work lies in its effects or what it produces, rather than seeing it as intrinsically valuable. *See also* intrinsic value; utilitarianism.

Z

zygote. The double, or diploid, cell formed by the union of the male sperm cell and the female ovum at conception. As a diploid cell, the zygote has twice the number of chromosomes as a normal germ cell. The zygote formed as a consequence of human reproduction is at the center of several ethical issues, including but not restricted to the question, "When does a human life begin?" Biblical passages such as Psalm 139 are often invoked to suggest that God has an intimate involvement with human beings even in the womb. Consequently, the zygote is generally considered uniquely human in the Christian view of life. *See also* abortion; bioethics; cloning; life, sanctity of; sexuality, sexual ethics; test tube babies.